PIANOS–
CARE AND RESTORATION

PRACTICAL HANDBOOK SERIES
Integrated Circuits: How to Make Them Work
by R. H. Warring

Clocks and Clock Repairing
by Eric Smith

Pianos – Care and Restoration
by Eric Smith

PRACTICAL HANDBOOK SERIES

PIANOS—CARE AND RESTORATION

by

ERIC SMITH

LUTTERWORTH PRESS
GUILDFORD AND LONDON

First published 1980

Eric Smith is also the author of:

PIANOS IN PRACTICE, AN OWNER'S MANUAL

(Scolar Press, London, 1978)

ISBN 0 7188 2436 6

Printed and Bound by
Butler & Tanner Ltd, Frome and London

CONTENTS

LIST OF PLATES

(The plates fall between pages 128 and 129)

LIST OF DIAGRAMS

INTRODUCTION

The player of a wind or bowed instrument pays far more attention to its welfare than the average home pianist pays to the condition of his or her piano. The piano is, of course, a more stable instrument, but it is rather surprising in this 'do-it-yourself' age that more owners do not take a practical interest in their pianos – granted, that is, that they are practical people in other areas. In some ways, this has redeeming features, for the piano, by its value in some instances, by the tensions in its structure, by its complexity and the delicacy of many interacting adjustments, stands somewhat apart from most other domestic instruments. There may be more at stake to be lost by blind poking and turning of screws, and certainly the piano is an instrument in whose servicing experience and an intuitive sense count for much.

But there is more than prudent caution involved. The piano is surrounded – some may say protected – by an aura, a mystique. Some of this may derive from the great era of the piano when, in the home, it was often a ladies' instrument, and ladies had servants and tradesmen ('craftsmen' would hardly be recognized) do the manual and maintenance work – though the ladies of an earlier age had tended their own clavichords. Some of it is due justly to the value and intricacy of the instrument. But now the piano is less an appurtenance of the finishing school, and indeed the ladies themselves see things differently. Amateurs in other fields do work on valuable and complex mechanisms and duly appreciate that the finer adjustments verge on the subjective and cannot be presented by formula or executed with mechanical exactitude alone. Skilled crafts are being revived everywhere by non professionals, whilst it is yet recognized that the expert must be called in for his or her experienced skill or other support.

I see this book as for the musician with a practical interest in pianos, and with some ability and inclination for practical work with the many materials that make up a piano. If a large

11

reason for the vogue of 'do-it-yourself' is economic — as, for example, in attending to the car or the decorations — this is not primarily a 'do-it-yourself' book. Except insofar as you may well decide to restore an instrument yourself which you could not afford to have restored professionally, or which the profession has refused to touch, the object is not to cut running costs or to reduce servicing or to make you less dependent on your professional consultant — though some of these may happen. The object is more to enable you to perform what a tuner, for one reason or another, may fail to do, or what he cannot do as often as you require, it is partly to help you towards the very great satisfaction to be found in working on pianos, and partly to enable you to improve your musical experience and to gain in appreciation of the instrument. This work involves many crafts in themselves rewarding, but the real reward is in using those crafts to produce a refinement which only the musician can fully enjoy. It is arduous work restringing a piano, although the process can be enjoyed; but the real satisfaction comes when you have the new strings reasonably stable and first begin to hear an acceptable tonal result of your labours. We shall be thinking of an intricate machine, and many people find intricate machines themselves to be of interest; but I have in mind such a person whose fundamental aims and standards are musical.

In my view there is no reason for, and no room for, enmity between the professional tuner/technician and the owner who feels obliged to adjust his or her own piano or to restore other instruments — provided that such a person preserves respect for the full-timer and does not, without a great deal of self-scrutiny as to his or her own merits, risk taking business from the professional. A professional can recite appalling instances of uninformed dabbling. I have seen some myself. But the way to avoid such catastrophes is to try to inform, for you cannot stop people from trying to help themselves and I believe that you should not attempt to do so. The role of the informed and practically-interested amateur is supplementary to that of the professional and not in conflict with it. Indeed, as one's response to the instrument develops with practical experience, one may well call on the tuner more rather than less; and that because one's own standards rise rather than because of nasty accidents.

Nonetheless, there are important cautions. Only you can assess the risk of offending and possibly losing your tuner. You must decide how far you are prepared to learn from your own piano and how far it may be practicable or desirable to pick up a 'banger' for experimental purposes – unless of course it is such a martyred instrument that you own already. It is most important for relations with the industry that you do not do imperfect work, with substitute materials, on other people's pianos whether or not for payment. It is far better to admit your limitations and restrict yourself to activities where enquiries of the professionals have met with a negative response than to bring the amateur into disrepute. Secondly, do not underestimate the task – even in simple terms of the space and endurance which may be needed. You can probably imagine the problem of getting 88 notes into a more or less mathematical series of pitches if you have cause to put the piano right out of tune. Envisage also the amount of reasonably dry space, the period of time, the volume of dirt and the sheer physical demands involved in overhauling a piano fully. Some jobs require more than one person, most work requires clear floor and storage space and even so apparently restricted a task as tuning can make intolerable demands of the human spine.

This book considers only 'straight' pianos – it omits electric pianos, mini-pianos where the action is below keyboard level, and the playing apparatus of player-pianos, although much of what is said will apply to these types also. There are chapters on tools and materials, on tone and touch and on tuning and toning, but the main part of the book is the sections on structure and resonant parts, on actions, and on keyboards. Each of these sections has a space devoted to repairs and adjustments. Some more general questions of buying or acquiring an old piano and restoring it are considered in the last chapter. Pianos have a specialized and not wholly standardized terminology which I have tried to use consistently but which may differ from what you might read elsewhere. The Glossary of Terms at the end of the book is intended to lessen such difficulties.

The diagrams are generally diagrams, not scale drawings. I hope that they help you to find your way about. The photographs of actions are, however, of real actions with only slight modifications (not affecting regulation) to make them fully visible. I hope that they give a clearer picture than diagrams of how piano actions work. The oscillograms are used purely for their illustrations of rather difficult concepts; for various reasons an oscilloscope is not in fact of much practical use in servicing and restoration of pianos, although experiment with it is of interest.

I should like to acknowledge once again the help I have received from Dr. and Mrs. A. J. Allnutt in producing the photographs and the oscillograms. They gave time, patience and expertise with extraordinary generosity. I am also grateful for the forbearance of my wife and family as pianos take over the house, a thick layer of dirt covers all, and single notes are struck *ad infinitum* into the small hours of the night.

Chapter One

TOOLS AND MATERIALS

Piano servicing and repairing are carried out largely by professionals at the present time and their world is somewhat jealously guarded. Some retail shops will take on repair and full restoration from the public, as will some makers, but their custom is secured mainly through tuners as intermediaries. Qualified tuners have of course practical technical experience but naturally some are more interested than others in adjustment and repair, and shops which undertake restoration vary as to what they do themselves and what they sub-contract. Sometimes, for example, they prefer to have whole actions rebuilt by specialist firms, by the action factory or the piano factory (since most piano-makers do not make their own actions any more than they cast their own iron frames). This then is a rather exclusive world of specialists fed by other specialists. The outlets for materials and tools often do not take kindly to amateur enquiries which may be ill-informed or result in small and time-consuming orders.

There is no denying that the situation is difficult, but as amateur interest in this field grows it is likely to improve. Some firms listed in the Directory (included in this book's Bibliography) will prove helpful, there are occasional advertisements in *Exchange and Mart*, and library research may produce other sources. If you require the correct materials you are likely to have to accept placing an order for larger quantities than your immediate needs. The alternatives are to confine yourself to work not requiring replacement material or to do your best (bearing in mind always the instrument's value and ownership) with substitute materials. There is still scope for improving a basically sound piano or for restoring a derelict instrument within these limitations.

TOOLS

With regard to tools, the absolute essentials can be obtained

15

from good music shops, tool and hardware shops as appropriate, and others can often be made up from material readily available. There is of course a wealth of gadgetry for particular specialist jobs, but most of these can be carried out more slowly without such labour-saving devices. The use of some of the tools mentioned will not be immediately apparent but will be explained in later chapters.

As a basic outfit for adjustments (Plates 1a and 1b), you need a tuning lever (also called a tuning hammer), a tuning fork and possibly a pitch pipe, at least a pair of mutes, a variety of screwdrivers, and several slotted tools which you can make. A spiral 'pump' screwdriver is useful for the many repetitive screwing jobs. Brass wire brushes (as for suede shoes) are useful for cleaning action woodwork and a dental mirror is helpful for glimpsing the inaccessible.

Tuning levers come in 'T'-shape and goose-neck shape, the latter being more widely available. Which you use is a matter of personal preference – some tuners feel the downward pressure of a T lever is better with a grand piano, but it is not essential. Modern sockets will not always fit the older tuning pins, but it is possible to adapt small socket spanners for the purpose, fitting new handles of steel rod or filing the driven end to fit the existing head of your tuning lever. Probably the most useful tuning fork is 'A–440' (being at the 'concert pitch' of 440 cycles a second) and however limited your ventures into tuning you should have one of these as a standard. You may also find it helpful to have a pitch pipe – like a mouth-organ – of chromatic notes for an octave in the middle range of the piano. These can be obtained from music shops, but do not buy a guitar-tuning pitch pipe as its range will not be suitable. Mutes are wedges of felt or rubber, being about 15 mm wide, 10 cm long and tapering to a point down from about 25 mm at the thicker end. If you cannot obtain the genuine article it is possible to make substitutes from hard felt polishing buffs (sold as accessories for electric drills) and even from rubber shoe-heels. The rubber wedges sold for holding sash windows are also usable. Generally felt of the right texture silences better than rubber and causes less of a 'thud'. The essential is for the mute to silence musical vibrations and to stay in place; home-made mutes are satisfactory but may give rise to distracting noise. There is a special type of expanding mute, looking rather like scissors, and muting two strings at a time; this Papp mute is not essential but it does make muting uprights easier since it can be inserted between the hammer shanks and rest on the hammer rail rather than slipping out into the depths of the piano. As for screwdrivers, you will need a large one – say 35 cm with a 15 mm blade – for work on cases and frames, one or two in-between sizes for general work, and a long narrow-bladed screwdriver for reaching into actions. Finally, a thin rod – say 20 cm by 2 mm – or a hexagonal nut spanner of about 5 mm may be needed to adjust capstans on keys; these vary in form but generally these tools or long-nosed pliers will turn them without damage.

The slotted tools are used in adjusting actions – regulating; particularly for bending fixed wires and springs and for turning the eyelet or stub-headed screws by which the escapement of the action is adjusted. You could make them up from steel rod (about 5 mm) as you go along, but for most regulating you will probably find useful a long (20 cm) right-angled lever with a slot 3 mm wide and about 1 cm deep. The slot can be made with a hacksaw and if necessary shaped with another saw or fine file. It is also possible to make a slot in an old screwdriver for this purpose, but the angle of the lever in the other tool can be helpful when regulating uprights. A slotted tool of a rather peculiar shape can be formed from similar material so that – after considerable practice – it can be used for adjusting uprights' damper spoons without removing the action from the piano; such a tool can also be bought and its use will be apparent later.

A special tool is useful for adjusting the dampers of grands (which can be done only with the action out of the piano). It can be made from a wooden block of about 10 cm long and 25 mm square, with a hole in the middle of the length. Through the hole goes a countersunk bolt some 7 cm long, and there is a fairly stiff coiled spring between block and wing-nut washer. The nut holds in place, but at adjustable height, a strip of material (wood, or metal or plastic) 3 mm thick and about 5 cm by 7 cm. (The only really critical dimension for this tool is that the slip be 3 mm thick as this an essential distance in regulating the dampers.) This gadget, as we shall see, is a means of relating the height of the dampers to the ends of the grand keys even though the action is out of the piano.

17

When you pass from tuning and general regulating to toning — working on the hammer heads — you need a few other tools. First and foremost are toning needles and holders. Commercial holders contain a row of three miniature clamps into which the needles are fastened. You can, however, get on perfectly well with darning needles in a good pin vice; using a single needle to tone a whole piano is a long and arduous business, but on the other hand it does reduce the very great danger of irretrievable damage being done to hammer felts by excessive needling — it compels the whole process to be as slow and gradual as it should be. If you are going to do any reshaping of hammers — and with old and unattended pianos this is hardly avoidable — you need to make up sand-files from various grades (centring on Medium) of sandpaper stuck with contact adhesive round strips of wood of convenient size — about 5 mm by 1 cm by 25 cm long, but the size is not critical. For other work on felt throughout the action and keyboard you need a very sharp knife — a trimming knife for which you can buy sets of blades is best — and a metal straight-edge. If, as may be, you cannot obtain commercial felt buttons or washers (used extensively beneath keys), you will have to make a great many to build up required thicknesses. An adjustable leather punch will make the central holes. For making the felt discs it is possible to construct a cutter from steel tubing with the outside edge ground sharp, the length being about 25 mm. The sizes most often used are 1 cm and 2 cm. Cutters made in this way should be hardened by heating to bright red and plunging into cold water. They are then used by compressing stacks of felt against them in a vice, with a soft jaw of wood used as a backing for the felt. A dowel plug-cutter in a hand drill can also be used for cutting felt discs.

Stringing requires special tools. You should have a smallish pair of top-cut nippers for cutting the softer wires used in piano actions. These cutters will be badly damaged if you try to use them on the piano wire used for strings; for this job you must obtain nippers with hardened blades and preferably with cantilevered handles — your tool shop will advise you if you explain that they are needed solely for cutting hard steel wire. Strong pliers are also needed — do not waste money on cheap ones with poor joints. Pliers with rounded jaws are very useful for bending tight curves in wire. It is desirable for the coils of strings on tuning pins to be touching each other and they do not always come out that way unaided. Therefore it is worth having a special lifting lever. This you can buy or make out of bent steel strip about 3 mm thick, shaped and notched with a file, and it should be backed with a slip of hard leather so that it does not scratch the frame. Make it 1 cm wide so that you can cut in the other end three equally-spaced slots which you will use to secure even spacing of the strings, or cut another strip for this tool. For knocking in tuning pins you need a fairly heavy hammer – say 2 lb. It is better to avoid claw hammers because of the risk of damage by the claw, and a fairly short haft is conducive to accuracy. A lighter hammer will be needed around the case and action and for tapping strings into place. If you have a torque wrench then regard it as available for work on pianos, for it is a useful accessory if you fit it with a socket which will grip tuning pins, but an expensive and inessential item.

Whilst adjusting pianos is not entirely a matter of scientific measurement, you need a good measure with clear fine divisions (for example a steel ruler), you can make use of a feeler gauge (mainly for internal comparison so whether or not metric in style does not matter), and a micrometer is valuable for measuring wire gauges; however, the micrometer is a luxury like the torque wrench and you can always present samples of the string to be replaced if the need arises. Certain gauges can perfectly well be home-made (*see* Fig. 1). For example, you need a strip of metal or wood 50 mm long, as this is the average standard distance which a piano hammer should be from the strings when at rest and it must be accurately measured if the piano is to give of its best. Another valuable gauge is for measuring key-dip – the distance which a key travels from 'up' to 'down'. This can be a small block, the width of a white key and 10 mm thick at the front, tapering to nothing at the back and 50 mm long. The height of the black keys ('sharps') above the white keys can be set with an 'E'-shaped piece of metal or thin wood. This height is normally 7/16 in or 12 mm above the white keys, so make your gauge with outside legs of about 30 mm length, with some 25 mm between them, and make the middle leg only 18 mm in length. In use, the outer legs stand on the white keys and the height of the intervening sharp is adjusted until it just touches the middle leg. A similar gauge, but with legs of equal

19

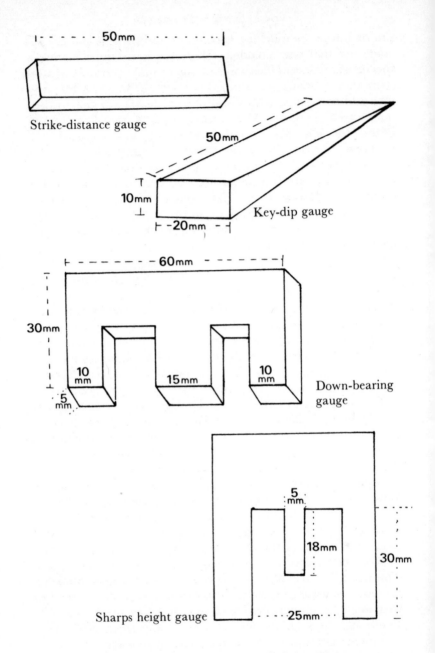

Fig. 1. Some home-made regulating gauges

length and of material (preferably metal) 5 mm thick, can be used with the feeler gauge to measure the important angles ('bearing') which the strings make relative to the top surface of the bridges.

A professional metal trolley for moving pianos is very expensive, but some form of trolley will soon be found necessary. A reasonable one can be made of heavy boards (say 25 mm) screwed together to double their thickness and mounted on four industrial-type castors – light domestic castors are unsuitable and dangerous. The wood can be about 25×45 cm. Cover the wood with carpet to protect the instrument, or with rubber to prevent it from slipping.

This may seem a formidable list of tools, but I have tried to indicate that the essentials are not in fact very many. There is no reason at all why you should buy or make at the outset all tools needed for a full overhaul, even if you are sure that the piano requires such extensive attention. The work takes a great deal of time and you can acquire and make more tools as they come to be needed. Most jobs can be done without specialist tools – they simply take longer and try your patience more. Perhaps I may repeat here that an oscilloscope is not only inessential but is actually unlikely to be of any use to you in normal servicing and restoration work.

MATERIALS

In materials, the prime requirements are glues and felts. You need a strong wood-glue – Scotch glue in block or granule form for melting in a double pot has many advantages but of course is not always convenient. Many modern cold glues are quite satisfactory as adhesives but have the disadvantage that they are difficult to soften should the parts have to be separated in future. For felt not under strain a more flexible glue, which will not be absorbed yet not create a hard surface, is desirable. Here Copydex serves well and is easily removable if need be. Impact adhesives are useful for quick repairs but are not very satisfactory with absorbent fabrics or always strong enough for wood. Epoxy finds a special use in filling bridges and soundboards. It occupies too much space to be useful for much else and is, again, hard to remove. The use of the various cyanoacrylate 'superglues' is not recommended. They do not work well on wood or fabrics and they will not stand up to the strains imposed on piano metalwork. They are in addition very difficult indeed to remove without damage to an underlying surface.

If you can obtain commercial felts, start by ordering 3 mm check felt (hard and close), 4–5 mm cushion felt (soft and open), and such damper and hammer felt as you may need. Sheet felts are sold by weight and 1 lb of each sort will keep you going for some time. For some purposes good close felt from a draper may be used, although more than one layer may be needed (it is usually not more than 2 mm thick). The back of the key-frame – i.e. the wood beneath the back ends of the keys – and the hammer rail (on which the heads of uprights' hammers rest) are usually covered with a thick green, very loose, felt known as baize, but it is possible to build up to the thickness here and for key punchings from several layers of thin felt. For small pieces, notably dampers, some chiropody felt is suitably thick and soft. True damper felt is sold in strips of the three common shapes and sheets for the rectangular dampers towards the top of the piano. (*See* Chapter 4.) There is a larger size for dampers of grand pianos. If you can obtain this damper felt cut to shape, it does a better job and looks tidier than any substitutes.

Hammer felt for hand covering can still be obtained, although machine covering is certainly preferable. (*See* Chapter 7.) The felt comes in tapered sheets, of a width greater than that of the piano, and in various weights, ranging from 3 lb per sheet to 8 lb per sheet. The 3 lb felt has a thickness of approximately 8 mm in the bass, and the 8 lb a maximum thickness of about 13 mm. The latter is for the heavy hammers of grands. If you buy from a felt processor you may be able to specify the thickest felt required and have a sheet specially pressed. When ordering felt you have naturally to estimate (with a slight allowance for wear and compression) the original maximum thickness of felt used to cover the bottom bass hammer. This felt is expensive, but so is having hammers covered by machine. You are likely to have to buy a whole sheet and this will cover the hammers of half a dozen pianos. There is no satisfactory alternative for recovering a whole run of hammers by hand. It is possible to deal with occasional hammers by using industrial felt deeply softened (again, this may be obtained from polishing buffs or some other domestic source), or chamois leather in the extreme treble (where the original felt may well be worn right through).

There are a number of miscellaneous materials which may or may not be needed. Wound strings can be had only from suppliers or manufacturers. Spring steel 'piano wire' for the uncovered strings – i.e. most of the piano – is, however, available at or through hardware or tool shops and is satisfactory for an unexceptional piano. It is usually held in Standard Wire Gauge. This covers the range of Music Wire Gauge, but in less fine steps. Therefore you must measure the original strings' thicknesses and replace as nearly as possible to the same size since any departure will result in tensions for which the particular instrument was not designed. Key coverings can be had in sets from suppliers together with adhesive, but it is worth looking around do-it-yourself shops for suitable white plastic strip with which to make isolated repairs as this can sometimes be all that is needed. Tapes (for upright actions) can be had from suppliers, as can their tips, but you may well find a suitable fine tape in a draper's and can stick to it hand-made tips of real or imitation leather. You need a small supply of several gauges of steel, and possibly brass, wire for making replacement springs in the action. Replace with similar material and gauge whenever possible.

For work on cases you will need the materials suggested in any book on french polishing – most older cases are french polished, although you may change the finish – and possibly some veneer; consult a work on restoration of furniture and finishing of wood to decide just what you need for a particular job. There are also some 'household chemicals' – ammonia, vinegar, methylated spirits – which you are almost bound to need as solvents or for thinning various polishes, varnishes and glues. Metal polish and a block of tripoli (from a hardware shop) come in handy, partly for polishing brass fittings, but also for use on non-metallic surfaces. Bronze, grey and black paints may be used (with a brush or from an aerosol) for restoring frames. Hammerite gives a pleasant and durable finish and dries quickly. The one thing for which you will find very little use (in the piano) is oil – there are few places in a piano where oil does anything but harm since it swells wood and retains dust.

The commonest lubricant is graphite powder, which you can obtain by rubbing a carpenter's pencil on the small parts, but which is best bought ready for use in a 'puffer' – hardware shops sell graphite in this form for lubricating locks. Do not, however, apply the 'puff' – a little goes a long way.

As with tools, the list is quite long – and indeed could be longer for particular projects – but you will see that the essentials are not difficult to obtain with the possible exception of felt. Appropriate felt is important to the instrument's tone and to the avoidance of wear and noise. It also does a good deal for appearance. Some sources of substitute material have been indicated and you may well find others, but remember that they *are* substitutes; there is some scope for experiment, but the proper place for it is not someone else's piano or an instrument of potential value.

Chapter Two

TONE AND TOUCH

Whilst in this book we concentrate on the mechanism and adjustment of the instrument, we should try to keep in mind always the musical objective of producing what no other instrument can produce, a distinctively pianistic sound. Of course part of this distinctive character depends on performance, sounds emitted in sequence, with rhythm, and with subtle relationships to each other. Yet all this would not be possible if the individual note did not have the desired properties. We must then first give a little thought to the nature of pianistic sound and how it is produced. If it does no more, this may provoke a critical listening habit, which is essential if you are trying to improve pianos.

TONE

Plate 2a gives a visual equivalent of a middle-range piano note, played at medium volume and with the note held down after playing. It would be an exaggeration to say that no other instrument could produce exactly this oscillogram, but the oscillogram reasonably illustrates one sound from a piano and its important features. The picture shows sound waves, the compressions and rarefactions of air produced by a vibrating string, amplified by a soundboard and transmitted by the air to the ear. The width of the wave – the distance between two high points – indicates the frequency of the wave which is equivalent to the pitch of the note (for this to be visible here would however require an enlargement of a picture taken over a much shorter period). In fact we know that the pitch of the note is Middle C with a frequency of 262 Hertz (cycles per second), and so we do not need to try to calculate it from the horizontal scale and the speed of the moving spot. On the vertical scale, the height and depth of the wave indicate the volume, or amplitude of the string's vibration – on the screen it of course depends on the amplification applied to the input, but is consistent for one

25

picture. This illustration represents a period of only two seconds – the sound was audible long after the picture was taken, but to show the whole sound would result in a reduction of scale which would obscure certain features.

Onset and Decay

The most important points to note are that the amplitude is not constant while the note sounds, and that the wavelength (in reality several wavelengths as we shall see) varies. In no sense is the note of a piano, however well tuned, constant. The whole distinctive rise-and-fall pattern of the picture represents what is called the 'tone envelope' of the sound. The vibrations before the sound reaches its peak amplitude are known as the 'onset' (here taking some 0.04 of a second), whilst the tailing off is known as the 'decay' of the note. In fact no sound simply starts and stops, to our perception, and the nature of any sound's rise and fall is an essential part of its distinctive character. This is particularly true of the onset even though in the case of a piano note, it occupies only a fraction of a second.

A sound without its appropriate onset characteristics is like a word made meaningless without any consonants. In the piano there is always a certain amount of noise from the works – the action – by which the key moves the hammer, though relative to tonal output this is low compared with what it is in some other instruments (the harpsichord, for example). Ignoring this, what produces the typical onset (which varies according to pitch) is the noise immediately as the hammer strikes the string, the resistance of the string to movement, movement between hammer and string since the string is straight but the hammer moves in a circular path, and the tendency of the string to vibrate in parts as it gets under way as a whole. These partial vibrations ('onset transients') are related to the wavelength of the string's vibration as a whole, and it is the excitation of partials in a particular order and at particular strengths which gives the characteristic onset to the note. The prominence and nature of the transients varies from instrument to instrument, depending on the length of the string and the hardness of the felt hammer head in particular, but pianos which are in reasonable order will go a long way to telling you that a single note heard in isolation (say, on a record or tape) emanates from a piano and not, for example, from a guitar or even from an electronic synthesizer. Cut out the onset, and the remaining sound will be very hard to identify.

What then of decay? Perhaps the most significant things are how soon it occurs after maximum vibration and how long it continues. For this conveys one paradox of the piano which is at the heart of its appeal – it is technically a percussive instrument with a very short onset, and yet it seems to be able to 'sing' (i.e. particularly to sustain). In fact of course the piano cannot sustain beyond the natural duration of vibration, since a string is set into vibration once and then left to do what it can unaided by any further excitement. The most that can be done is to remove whatever interferes with free vibrations, notably the dampers. Moreover, power and its sustaining are in inverse proportion; had it not to vibrate the huge soundboard to amplify, the string would be able to vibrate for very much longer, and these factors have to be balanced in design. Decay begins almost immediately, though with decreasing speed as we go down the scale, even when a key is held down. The sustaining power, such as it is, varies very much from instrument to instrument. Generally the bigger the piano and the longer its strings, the lower is its natural resonant pitch and the longer it will sustain. This natural resonant pitch depends on the design and materials of the instrument; it is the 'formant' which dictates the characteristic tonal potential of any particular instrument. Grands do not differ very much from uprights (in these respects) save that of course grands, apart from 'baby grands', are bigger. As the precise moment when the note starts is virtually indefinable, so is the moment when it dies. By way of example, however, the duration of clearly audible sound from a 2 m grand struck hard, with the key held down, was found to be 29 seconds (Bottom C), 20 seconds (Middle C) and 3 seconds for the Top C. The proportions are indicative though the exact figures have no significance. Thus the oscillogram in Plate 2a represents only about one-tenth of the total period of this note's audible decay.

Another factor to be borne in mind about decay is that it is compounded by ambient reverberation and echo and, even in the most acoustically 'clean' surroundings, a note played staccato still decays, if rapidly, rather than being totally cut off. Plate 2b shows the same Middle C played with the shortest possible staccato, and its period of decay is quite apparent. Here the oscillogram shows virtually the whole duration of sound, about half a second, and is on the same time-base as in Plate 2a. (The straight line after the steep decay is the width of the oscilloscope beam and does not represent audible sound to any significant extent.) This imperfection of staccato arises partly because no piano damper can immediately and completely silence all vibration in the string, and partly because the sound-board, frame and case are not directly acted upon by the damper and so continue to vibrate when the string has been stilled.

This characteristic is particularly noticeable with the long single strings of the bass in a piano, for obvious reasons; they represent a larger mass to bring to a halt, the dampers tend to bounce on them and the inherent resonance of the instrument is nearest in wavelength to that of the longer strings. The effect in the extreme bass is clear from Plate 3a, representing Bottom C played staccato. A fast staccato passage in the extreme bass is rarely met; if you try one as an exercise you will find it hardly meaningful in terms of staccato, for the notes decay into each other and in any case the ear finds these low frequencies hard to distinguish. The duration near full amplitude in this picture is some 0.4 seconds. The full duration of the decay is lost in the width of the beam, but is at least 2 seconds.

Plate 3b (which for convenience is still on the same time-base) shows Bottom C played with the key held down. Comparison with Plate 2a shows the lower note's longer wave-length (the greater separation of the peaks) and the much greater duration of the sound for a similar starting amplitude. We have here some 1.6 seconds of sound in which decay is very gradual indeed, and after that the note was audible for 24 seconds. Plate 3c demonstrates the very different envelope of a top note. The distinction will be recognized when it is known that a faster time-base was used so that, in comparison with the previous examples, the note appears longer than in fact it was. Initial noise bulks large in the whole sound, which has decayed almost beyond audibility in 0.003 seconds. There is of course no damper for this note; the staccato picture would be identical

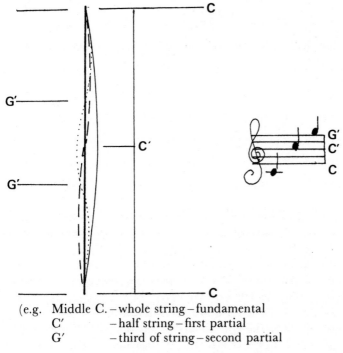

(e.g.   Middle C. –whole string – fundamental
        C′   – half string – first partial
        G′   – third of string – second partial

Fig. 2. Fundamental and first two partials

and even were a damper present it could have no sensible effect on so short a period of sound.

Partials

It has been said that the onset is characterized by a mass of 'partials' of transient duration. However, also during the maximum sound period the string vibrates in parts and these are mathematical proportions of the string, with frequencies of vibration also proportionate. They may be referred to as 'partials', 'harmonics' or 'overtones' (*see* Fig. 2). Strictly speaking, a harmonic is an integral multiple of its fundamental's frequency, whereas a partial is not necessarily so related. We shall call all secondary vibrations partials – an unmusical word, but one which makes it clear that we are excluding the fundamental frequency of the whole string; for example, the first partial (often known as the second harmonic, because it is the product

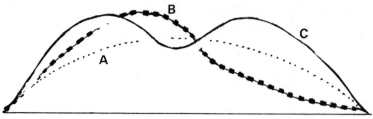

A. Fundamental (half-cycle)
B. Fundamental with 1st partial
C. Fundamental with 2nd partial

Fig. 3. Wave-forms of fundamental with partials

of the second longest vibrating length of string) is twice the frequency of the fundamental and is the sound which you receive
if you limit the string exactly in the middle.

Partials are represented on an oscillogram, but not in isolation – any more than as a rule they are heard in isolation
(though in some instruments they may be). To make a full harmonic analysis of even a good oscillogram is no easy matter,
but you can assess the complexity or simplicity of a note's harmonic structure in general terms. Plate 4 shows an almost pure
sine wave of Middle C. This is in fact from the 8 ft flute of an
electronic organ and too simple a sound ever to be heard on
a piano. A similar wave is produced by a tuning fork. With
a harmonically rich sound the wave forms of partials modify
the outline of such a fundamental wave pattern according to
how many times in the main vibration each partial occurs. Thus
the first partial occurs twice, being an octave higher, and introduces a dip in the main wave form so that it takes on the shape
of an escarpment – steep on one side, dented and gradual on
the other (Fig. 3). Add the second partial to the fundamental
and the wave takes a dip in the middle, becoming saddle-
shaped. And so the basic waveform is more and more complicated according to how many partials contribute to the total
sound – and according, visually, to the time-base of the oscilloscope which must be set very fast if a single fundamental wave
is to be examined.

The untrained ear can fairly well detect the first and second
partials – an octave, and an octave plus a fifth (C and G) –

above the fundamental (C in this case). If you hold Middle C down without letting it sound, then play the C above, staccato and loudly, you should be able to hear the higher C sound on the Middle C strings, for undamped silent strings are set in vibration by vibrating strings of related frequency. (This is part of what happens when you use the right hand 'sustaining' pedal.) But, on the whole, partials achieve their effect as determining the 'tone' of a note rather than as separately audible. As many as nine, in a series of proportionately increasing frequencies going upwards (the 'harmonic series'), may contribute significantly in this way – they contribute by division of the main string into vibrating parts when the corresponding strings are in fact damped, and still more markedly when the corresponding strings are undamped and so take up the vibrations of the main string's partials. The latter happens when the pedal is used, and also throughout the higher reaches where the strings have no dampers; this is quite significant since we reach these undamped strings with the seventh partial of the fundamental of E below Middle C, and thus the whole central range of the piano, in which 'cantabile' melodies are chiefly set, derives tonal benefit from the undamped treble strings. Equally, of course, the 'harmonic series' extends beyond the range of keyboard and strings, since the top string must produce its own partials, albeit faintly.

Now while it is not easy to make analysis of partials in a piano note, we do know some important facts. For example, the audible harmonic content becomes richer as we go lower in pitch but, correspondingly, the audibility of the fundamental becomes less. Indeed, some tuners tune the lowest strings by dividing them and tuning to the first or second partial above, since it is so difficult to hear accurately their fundamental frequencies. The middle range of the piano quite naturally offers a compromise between clear fundamentals and rich partials which is pleasing and not wearisome to the ear. The top offers less in the way of partial content, save that the unmathematical partials which are 'noise' bulk large in the total sound (as was noted in Plate 3c).

Pianos vary in the harmonic structure which they offer; the relative proportions of the fundamental and particular partials determine their 'tone', and this varies first for individual notes, then more generally for top, bottom or middle, and then more generally still for the instrument as a whole. The general impression of tone can only be the sum of impressions of individual notes (which, albeit, have also the factor of the combination with other notes in performance to be considered). Thus when we say that we like the 'tone' of a particular piano we are either talking loosely or performing a mental act of generalization which is exceedingly complex, being based on registering and comparing almost innumerable auditory data related to the particular instrument's formants and their effect at various pitches.

Tone and Volume

There is yet another factor of 'tone' of which we must be aware. Assuming that the action is appropriately adjusted and that you have a nearly mechanical touch so that you can cause each hammer to strike each string with the same velocity, you will produce from bass notes much more volume – tone, it may be said – than from the middle or extreme treble ranges. (We saw this in considering Plate 3b). It has long been a principle of piano design, mainly in the interests of stability, that the strings should be as nearly as possible all at the same tension. In that case a longer string will have a greater amplitude of vibration for a given blow; it is true that the strings differ substantially in mass, particularly where low bass notes have to be secured by heavy windings rather than by proportionate length of string, but by and large this is compensated for by a gradual increase in the mass of the hammers as you go down the scale, and adjustments are made to keep the touch weight fairly (not entirely) constant throughout the instrument. We have already noticed that the bass strings are richest in partials, and this is related to their greater amplitude of vibration. The greater amplitude you secure for these and other notes, the more partials – the richer (but not necessarily pleasanter) the tone which you generate. Thus it is perfectly natural that the 'loud' pedal may be said to modify tone and volume, since tone and volume are related. It does so, as, as we have seen, by permitting both the intermingling of sounds and partials and the excitement of partials whose strings have not actually been struck.

32

But tone and volume are related only to some extent. For there is the question of quality. 'Good' or 'pleasant' or 'mellow' (requirements tend to be subjective) tone is not that with the highest number of partials, but that with the pleasantest arrangement of them in varying strengths related to the fundamental. As you go up the harmonic series, the partials become more and more discordant to the fundamental frequency. In moderation, they brighten and enhance its tone, as do the 'mixture' stops on an organ, but in excess they create a displeasing sound. We cannot switch them in and out during performance as on an organ; we must find a good compromise tone for all occasions. Moreover, we have to remember that volume is not absolute for musical purposes although of course intensity of sound can be objectively measured. A 'cantabile' melody is played very smoothly, somewhat louder than its accompaniment, and its tone 'sings'. Play it very loudly and it will cease to sing. Play it as loudly as at first, but the accompaniment more loudly, and again the melody will fail to sing. Tone and volume are relative and subjective things. There are areas of common agreement and preference but there are no absolute rules as to what in detail is 'good'. The ideal harmonic structure for every note of the perfect piano simply cannot be laid down.

Tone and Piano Hammers

Every piano has a threshold beyond which hitting it harder will produce partials to the extent of irregular 'noise', where the string can vibrate no more to add to the ordered sound which we call tone. (The ear, or brain, one may suspect as one listens to the children practising or even to the occasional lion of the keyboard, also has such a threshold.) This limit depends for any instrument on a multitude of factors in design and materials. These are for the most part in-built and barely capable of alteration, and they have a good deal to do with the value (monetary and musical) of different pianos. But one other factor which greatly influences tone is the condition of the hammers. Various materials in various conditions elicit different responses from the strings (granted that the comparison is made with hammers of the same mass). When we considered decay we noted that some features of the sound envelope depend on the fact that the hammer suddenly meets an inert mass,

33

the taut string. It then travels with, and minutely along, the string before bouncing back (or down, in a grand). Although all this happens very quickly, so does the whole onset, so that the dwelling of the hammer on the string is of significance and contributes to tone just as does the nature of the vibration which it has begun.

Obviously a relatively soft material striking the string is liable to linger whereas a hard substance bounces off at high speed. The soft material in fact acts as a damper for a brief moment, and what it damps is the upper partials. Thus a very soft, hammer, while it may not be soft enough to noticeably dampen the whole string, produces a fundamental with meagre partials. This can sound dull and muted. A hard hammer produces a wealth of partials which tend to obscure the fundamental, so that the result is bright and may be strident. The ideal hammer – the ideal condition, that is, for hammers are constantly changing in density – is somewhere in between. Close felt has been found for over a century to be the ideal covering. It contributes much (with highly tensioned strings) to distinctive piano tone as against the tones of earlier instruments which plucked or struck the strings with far harder materials (but had slacker strings).

The composition of a felt hammer is and has to be complex. The felt is shaped and strained round the hammer in such a fashion that the centre, close to the wood, is compressed hard, whilst a varying outer depth is by contrast stretched – if you sliced into a newish hammer it would burst open. The result is a body of felt which to a controlled extent damps as well as stirs the strings. As we shall see, the state of the felt almost right through can be varied and this, which calls for experience and fine judgment, has a very potent effect on the tone of the piano. You cannot introduce tonal qualities which the design and stringing militate against, but you can persuade the instrument as you have it to give of its best.

Plate 5 shows the same strings struck by hammers in various conditions, a mechanism being used to ensure that each blow was of the same velocity. The time-base of all these pictures is the same. Plate 5a represents a very soft hammer felt – note the sustained regularity of the waves. Plate 5b is of a pleasantly toned hammer felt, richer and more complex than the previous

34

sound. The third picture is from a very hard old felt in which the pattern is complicated by a mass of partials beating against each other – the undulating amplitude represents partials in various discord and concord (*see also* Plate 15).

TOUCH

Outline of the Action

We have noted how quickly tonal decay sets in and how tone and volume are related. These points predicate certain features of the piano action, the mechanism by which our fingers cause strings to vibrate – and also certain controversies about how and when the tone of a note is produced. What has to be remembered is that when the hammer meeets the string it travels by its own velocity, having ceased to have any mechanical connection with the finger of the player. The hammer is no different in this respect from a ball thrown at the string. Whatever the pianist may do, the hammer must (if the action is properly regulated) strike the string and then bounce off it, and the force with which it strikes the string depends on its mass, the leverage of the action, and the strength of key depression. Of these only the latter is variable and only minute variations can be imparted to the hammer (e.g. by accelerating depression or a constant rate) once it has been set in motion, variations which may have no effect on the end result, the speed of the hammer.

We shall be looking at the action more closely later, but at this stage it is worth having an outline of its behaviour in mind (*see* Fig. 4). For this purpose the grand and upright actions are similar. Besides the pivoted hammer there are three parts – the pivoted key, pivoted wippen, and the jack (a trigger – also known as the 'fly' or 'hopper' – which is pivoted to the wippen). The tip of the jack presses up against the butt end of the hammer and it is its movement which drives the hammer. The jack moves when the key raises the wippen as the front of the key is depressed. The hammer head usually travels 50 mm and the key-front 10 mm, so that the action directs the hammer in relation to key velocity in a ratio of rather less than 1 : 5 (less, because about 1 mm of key depression is merely follow-through, 'aftertouch'). Thus leverage is at work.

If this were all that happened, of course the hammer would

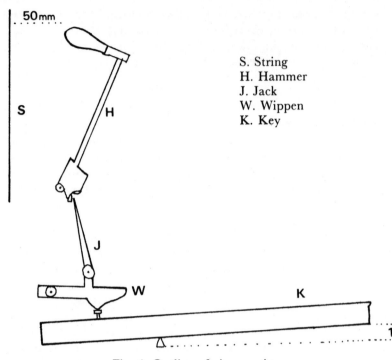

Fig. 4. Outline of piano action

stay on the string so long as the key were held down and the string would hardly vibrate at all. In fact an adjustable screwed regulating button is set to intercept the heel of the jack just (usually 2–3 mm) before the hammer reaches the string. So the jack is held, the hammer is quite free and strikes the string under its own velocity, whilst the key can be pressed further down without interfering with the hammer – the jack is merely pushed further from the hammer butt by the regulating button.

To this arrangement there are two refinements, one being the dampers on most strings (Fig. 5 – the upright version is shown) and the other being the check. The function of the damper is obvious and of course it must be controlled by the key, being activated by the wippen (upright) or by the key itself (grand). The function of the check is to catch the hammer when it bounces back, if the key is still partially depressed. If there were no check, the hammer would fall right back and the jack

36

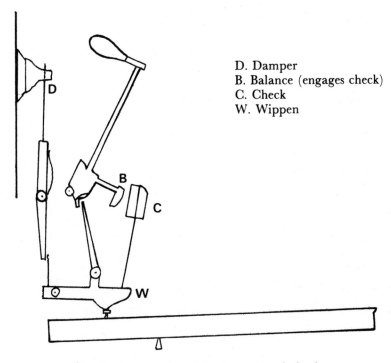

D. Damper
B. Balance (engages check)
C. Check
W. Wippen

Fig. 5. Outline of upright damper and check

would relocate for a fresh blow (if indeed it did so) only when the key were released. This would make fast playing and repetition impossible.

Touch and Tone Production

One of the most crucial and still controversial matters in this area concerns the nature of the power which a player exercises over the sound produced as he or she presses the keys. Just before impact the hammer cannot be under control or direct influence since manifestly it has no physical connection with the jack which alone can drive it (Fig. 6). But there are some who maintain that variations of touch during each depression do affect the way in which the hammer strikes the string and, consequently, the tone. It is rather as if the player could affect the hammer after it leaves the jack as the bowler can so manipulate the ball before it leaves his hand that its subsequent flight

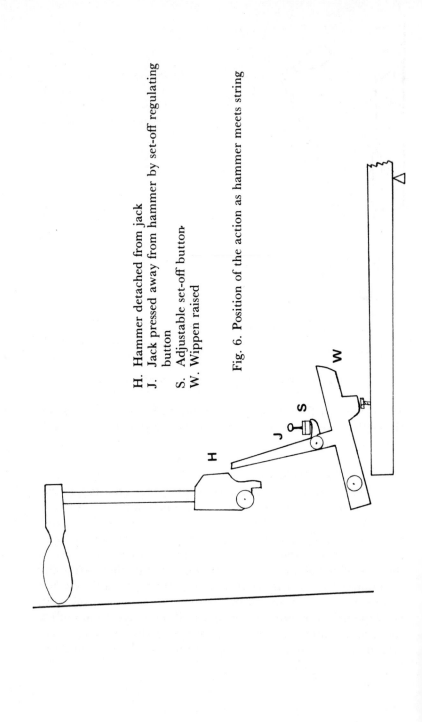

H. Hammer detached from jack
J. Jack pressed away from hammer by set-off regulating button
S. Adjustable set-off button
W. Wippen raised

Fig. 6. Position of the action as hammer meets string

is affected by its spin. My own feeling is that this capability for the piano – or pianist – is extremely doubtful. The time when the hammer is free is minute. The only variation possible is in the velocity with which it strikes the string and whatever means produces this variation cannot add any other characteristics to it; the speed of the hammer's leaving the jack is what counts and it continues to be the only variable, no matter what digital contortions the pianist may contrive. (The period for which the key is down and the damper up does of course vary and affect tone, as staccato varies from tenuto, but this is another matter from the speed of depression though the two may in practice be related.)

Nonetheless, I think it is rather too easy to belittle the other school of thought. It stems from a deep subjective experience of the inherent magic of the piano and its most ardent proponents have a profound sense of the mystery of their instrument. The psychology of attempting to achieve 'cantabile' tone (the commonest example) other than by simple gradation of force or volume, is not negligible. It is more, not less, remarkable that the piano can produce effects of such subtlety by complex variations merely of force. What we have seen to be fairly involved in the production of tone in one note is almost infinitely more so in chords and series of chords, especially when the sustaining pedal is introduced, and the speed and completeness of damping can certainly be varied by the speed of key return which has no necessary relationship to its initial depression. The direction on a piece to play in a certain manner, suggesting something other than speed or volume, concentrates the mind and cannot but influence the fingers even if in reality they are but accomplishing subtle and minute gradations of speed of depression. Schumann's favourite 'Innerlich' is an instance of such a direction which I feel certain must affect one's touch, although how it is to be effected one is not told and how it *is* effected one would find hard to define. Any one unit of the piano action is fairly simple. Eighty-eight such units, interrelated, are not at all simple. The connection between touch and tone has a certain mystery which is the true pianist's delight. We are not so much mixing metaphors as acknowledging something indefinable when we talk of making the percussive instrument 'speak' or 'sing'.

39

Heavy and Light Touch

We have now to think of touch not in the sense of your finger's pressure, but rather as the state of the action which requires a particular finger pressure to meet the minimum demand for the hammer to strike the string; 'touch' is understandably used of the instrument as well as of the player – and not always very distinctly. The feel of the keys to you is almost entirely conditioned by the mechanics in fact, but it is an important part of the subjective aspect of playing the piano in practice. At the lowest level – though even this is no simple matter to achieve – the touch must be predictable because if it is not the sound will not be predictable. As you play, you form an impression of the sound before you make it and you compare it at least to some extent with the sound which you actually create. There must be a strong probability that they will be essentially similar in character or you will get nowhere; and there has to be a consensus, an acceptable range, for all pianos although of course you are particularly able to predict the sound of a piano which you know well. At the very least, variations in touch should correspond to a series of true potentials in the compass of the piano so that the finger 'knows' what sound it will produce. The only way to secure this is to have every unit of the action 'regulated' the same, or regulated differently but by some rational principle, for example a heavier touch in the bass.

The heaviness or lightness of touch depends on several matters in any one unit. Moreover, when you look into it, the touch is not of a constant weight as you press a key – there are heavy and light spots according to what is being done at particular instants. You ideally want these spots to occur at exactly the same stage of key depression for each key. The heavy spots are the taking of the hammer's weight on to the jack (in an upright – in a grand it is there from the start), the raising of the damper, and the pressure of the regulating button on the jack's heel just before the 'escapement' of the jack from the hammer (Fig. 7). If you have pressed the key hard enough to get it past these moments so that the hammer can sound, you will hardly notice the light 'aftertouch', since it will be a millimetre of fast travel (although its absence would give a very tight, unyielding feeling and could make escapement and checking unreliable).

There is not much licence for determining the stage of depres-

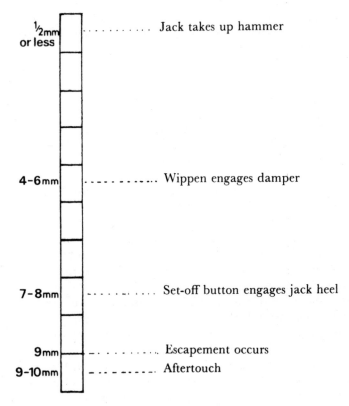

Fig. 7. Stages in upright key depression

sion at which escapement occurs. If power is not to be lost yet the hammer is not to stick ('block') on the string and damp its vibration, the action must be adjusted so that the hammer is very close to the string before it escapes and the key will be almost down, having ceased to drive at that point. The taking on of the hammer, again, should occur almost as the key is first touched, or energy will be wasted. But with the damper, some variation is possible. It must be well clear of the string when the hammer strikes. Equally, it must not rise when another note is sounding. Subject to this, variation is available and affects the feel of touch, though generally matters are adjusted so that the two weights of damper and of escapement are not taken on together.

41

There are also more pervasive factors affecting touch. The most obvious is the resistance of the action, which includes the dead weight of the hammers and wippens and also the friction in their pivots ('centres'). With the action properly adjusted, its weight is related to the keys so that the latter, of standard size, will require a weight of between 2 and 3 oz (60–80 g) to depress them. Note that this is with the dampers raised and excluded from the weight. The relation is usually secured by cylindrical lead weights, these being placed in the tails of the keys if the action is light and in their fronts if it is heavy.

Then, in the upright, there are the damper springs. These have a very marked influence on touch and are of two or three different strengths from treble to bass. If the touch is felt to be heavy, these springs can sometimes be replaced with lighter ones (or merely eased) without impairing the damping. However, this is not to be undertaken lightly and certainly not before the action has been properly regulated. Older actions used brass springs; if these are replaced with steel wire, a finer gauge will be needed. With grands the only simple way to lighten touch is to arrange for damping to be a little delayed (as can also be tried with uprights). Of course, with both instruments you can add or reduce key weights, but this is not advisable. The weights were set at manufacture for a designed touch with a particular action. To alter all of them is expensive, difficult, and a detraction from the carefully planned entity of the instrument; to alter one or two is to confess to being unable to find specific other faults which must be present. If you are dealing with a strange piano, remember that touch weight is strongly addictive and also that a new piano needs to be 'run in'. A sloppy action on an old piano of your own can persuade you that a new piano is 'heavy' when it is not, just as the new piano may require several months' playing. The requirement is almost always to lighten touch rather than to make it heavier, and one must be careful before deciding on such an undertaking. Lightening of the touch will inevitably affect the crispness of the keys' return and that is a serious disadvantage. The exception is where heavy touch is due to stiff action centres. This is not likely to be a consistent fault in an elderly instrument and in a new one will cure itself with time.

TOUCH AND TONE

Though its fact can be weighed and measured, taste in touch, like taste in tone, is ultimately subjective. Some players like a good resistance from the keys whilst others find it an obstacle. A very minute alteration in touch weight throughout the instrument will produce a very large change in its feel. Arbitrary as touch preference might be, it is not a trivial matter. There is no doubt whatever that tone is directly dependent on the touch of the pianist (just as that is related to the 'touch' of the instrument), given the potential of a certain instrument. The argument is not there, but as to *how* and by what means variations of touch can produce variations of tone.

We have seen that the variables involved in both touch and tone are very many even in one instrument, and of course they are still more when we compare instruments and take into account more than one player. If you know older keyboard instruments you will know that the clavichord produces fragile sounds with an enormous variety of tonal nuance within a low dynamic range. Its attraction, its expressiveness, is closely connected with the simplicity of its mechanism – the raised metal tangent at the back of the key strikes the string direct. The harpsichord, with a plucking action almost completely independent of touch variations, is more powerful but more complex and – even an admirer may say – veers towards the mechanical rather than the expressive, though there are ways of making its music more varied than superficially appears possible. The paradox is that the piano is even more complex mechanically, involves the movement of much greater masses, and has the finger even further removed from the string itself. Yet it has not only the harpsichord's power but also the clavichord's responsiveness (Fig. 8).

We have always to bear in mind this critical interaction of touch and tone when we work on pianos. They are highly wrought mechanisms, depending on the interplay of carefully balanced forces which are never entirely stable and are capable of producing effects opposite in character to the 'mechanical'. Yet they cannot produce them unless the mechanism is well adjusted and the sonorous parts of the instrument are in good order.

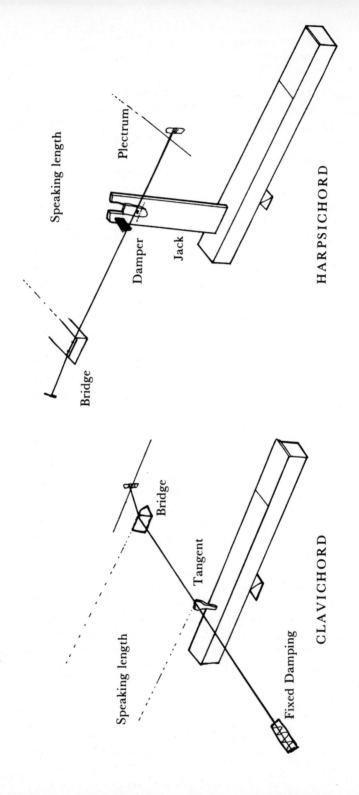

Fig. 8. Clavichord and Harpsichord actions

Chapter Three

STRUCTURE AND SOUND-PRODUCING PARTS

STRUCTURE AND CASE

Basic Structure

Normally the structural basis of the whole piano is the 'back', a framework constructed of stout timber (which may well be 10 cm or more in section) mortised together in the form of a surround with crossing beams or braces. The purpose of this is to support the soundboard and iron frame, with its tensions and great weight (*see* Fig. 9). In some slim-line uprights this back is very much reduced, there being no braces and the structural basis being the frame and thick surround to which it is screwed. Then the frame itself has to be strengthened and any increase here results in a sharp rise in total weight (usually for an upright in the region of a quarter of a ton, and for a medium grand perhaps one third of a ton) so that compromises have to be made.

The back supports also the side members of the case. In an upright these have minor acoustic importance, since the soundboard is fixed primarily to the heavy back. In a grand, the sides – one straight, the other a curved rim made of some ten hardwood laminations – have deep ledges supporting the soundboard and frame and the lower sides have the braces mortised into them well below the level of soundboard and frame. The soundboard edges are clamped down with a hardwood strip. As the whole structure is far more integral, it has also far more effect on tone (Fig. 10). The grand back is continued forwards into the bed, supporting the action and keyboard, whilst the wrestplank containing the tuning pins rests on wooden blocks at the sides and is screwed to the frame in the front. The lack of support for the grand wrestplank and frame at the front is an unavoidable weakness. The upright's wrestplank is glued and screwed firmly to the beam at the top of the back and the soundboard goes right up to it. The grand's soundboard must of course stop short

45

of the wrestplank so that the hammers can rise between – this also is an unavoidable defect (Fig. 11).

The sides of both models extend to the front in the form of curved 'cheeks' between which is situated the key-bed, a structural framework which is fairly massive in the grand since it carries the weight of keyboard and action and also indirectly of the front frame and wrestplank. In the upright the key-bed is less substantial and can usually be removed without difficulty for re-stringing and other purposes. Often it is supported in the middle by a cast bracket projecting from the frame and is screwed into the cheeks from below. Sometimes the cheeks have

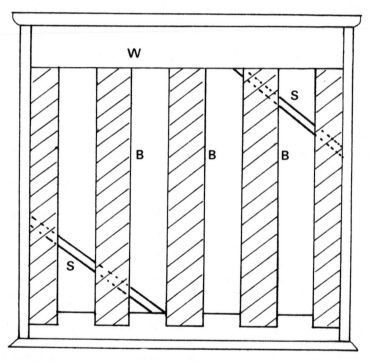

UPRIGHT

W. Wrestplank (with tuning pins) and top edge of soundboard
S. Cut away edge of soundboard if board
   does not cover whole back
B. Braces – design varies

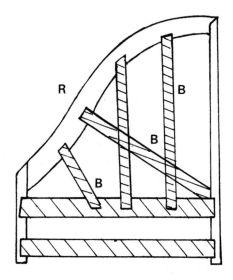

GRAND (*from below*)

R. Laminated hardwood
    curved rim
B. Braces – design varies

Fig. 9. Typical braced backs

to be removed from the sides together with the key-bed. The columns found at the front of older (and a few classic modern) uprights as a rule do not support the key-bed but are ornamental. On recent uprights the sides and cheeks may be finished as, or actually be, single pieces of wood or blockboard, but on older models the cheeks are separate and screwed into the sides, and this method also is still used. At the bottom of uprights is the 'bottom board', supporting the pedals and on older models usually glued and screwed to projecting 'toe-blocks' on which the columns stand. The weight is largely in the frame, but strong bottom corner joints are essential to prevent dangerous rocking backwards and forwards. Some modern uprights without good toe-blocks develop weaknesses here (Fig. 12). In the grand, the weight is of course spread over a larger area and is taken by three (occasionally six) legs, usually with some form of castor and often a brass cap. The legs are detachable by various devices for removal purposes, but take a great deal of strain if the instrument is pushed sideways. Square tapered legs have long been the fashion (save in reproduction models), but polygonal or round legs with ornamental grooves and turned or

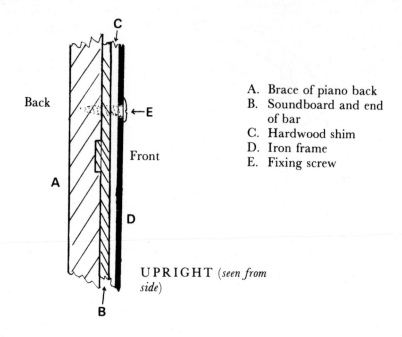

Back

Front

A. Brace of piano back
B. Soundboard and end of bar
C. Hardwood shim
D. Iron frame
E. Fixing screw

UPRIGHT (*seen from side*)

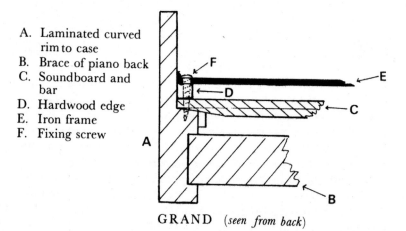

A. Laminated curved rim to case
B. Brace of piano back
C. Soundboard and bar
D. Hardwood edge
E. Iron frame
F. Fixing screw

GRAND (*seen from back*)

Fig. 10. Sections through sides

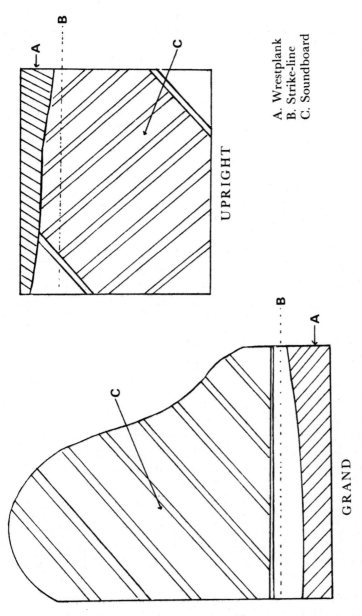

A. Wrestplank
B. Strike-line
C. Soundboard

UPRIGHT

GRAND

Fig. 11. Soundboards and strike-lines

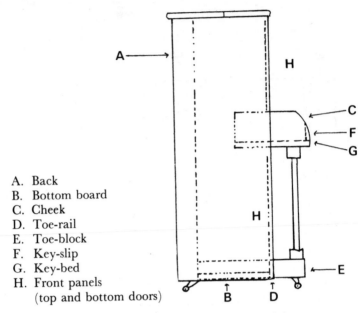

A. Back
B. Bottom board
C. Cheek
D. Toe-rail
E. Toe-block
F. Key-slip
G. Key-bed
H. Front panels
   (top and bottom doors)

Fig. 12. Case and structure of (older) upright

carved tops were usual until about the time of the First World War.

Fittings

There are various removable covers and fittings which have no structural importance and little, though sometimes adverse, acoustic effect. Music desks vary according to date rather than convenience. A really satisfactory and convenient music desk has yet to be devised. Desks of grands were often elaborately fretted until the First World War, then sometimes made with a few straight slats, and most recently take the form of a solid wooden panel. The latter blocks the sound and the former is contrary to modern taste; the slatted type has much in its favour. The desks are hinged to a ledge ending in side-shelves which slide in felted grooves let into the sides above the wrest-plank.

Desks of uprights, vintage and veteran, are hinged to the front panel and can be folded back into the top of the instrument. They have the drawback that they obstruct the 'fall' (the lid over the keyboard) when it is opened for playing and they tend to mark the front panel when they swing sideways. The more modern form is a ledge hinged inside the fall. This tends to be rather poor for holding music, especially if the front edge of the fall is not hinged and so catches the spines of music books, and may inadvertently be shut down on top of the keys. A recent attempt is a full-width desk worked into the hinged front of the fall. When the fall is opened, the front is folded down and reveals a grooved rest on its inner edge. This is neat, but the music tends to come too nearly vertical to the front panel and is unstable. Despite its inconvenience, the old swinging desk was the best arrangement purely from the point of view of holding music to be read. It is now very general not to fit the familiar clips for holding pages – in some designs there is little room for them. Sometimes rubber buttons are provided instead. Many pianists regret the passing of the clips and it is in fact quite possible to fit a pair for oneself on most types of desk.

The mounting of upright and grand falls differs greatly. In old uprights the fall is hinged to a concave beam well above the keys, down from its shape as the 'hollow'. The hollow slots into place between the cheeks and also receives the front panel, which is usually located with short dowels into holes in the hollow. Just below the hollow, and above the keys, is the 'nameboard', running full width, sometimes bearing the trade name (though this is often on the underside of the fall) and with a felt strip below it to prevent dust entering the case between the keys. Modern preference is for lighter and less curved arrangements. Sometimes the fall is hinged directly to the front panel, which extends down and may replace the nameboard. This can make removing the panel rather difficult. More often, a thinner wooden strip replaces the hollow. With the hollow it appears externally that the fall must cover half the keys when open as the piano-hinge runs down the middle. This is an illusion (though not always entirely so) arising from the use of deep keybeds. The old falls were curved, made of two or more shaped parallel strips glued together and with no hinge at the front edge. Nowadays falls are usually straight and reach back almost to the front panel, with the hinge virtually in the angle. As a rule, the front edges of these falls are hinged. Whilst there are other arrangements, the falls of grands usually pivot in slotted

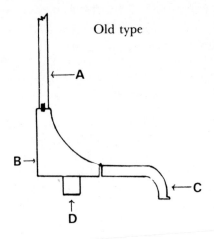

Old type

A. Front panel
B. Hollow
C. Fall
D. Nameboard
E. Notch for supporting
   dowel in cheek

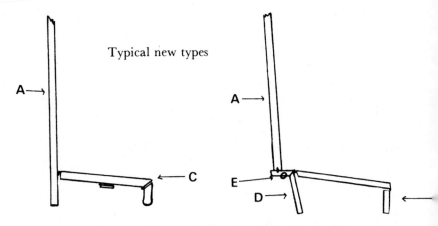

Typical new types

Fig. 13. Old and new upright fall arrangements

plates in the cheeks, so that they can generally be lifted out without any unscrewing. (*See* Fig. 13).

Both upright and grand have a strip of wood in front of the keys which conceals the keyframe and felts below the keys. As it often contains the lock, this is sometimes called the 'lock rail', but is more often known as the 'key-slip' (though this may also be a thinner strip behind the lock rail). The key-slip may be screwed in from underneath (uprights and grands), or held in place by rebated 'key-blocks' (most grands), in which case it may locate in the key-bed with dowels. In uprights it may be a fixture, since the key-frame can be lifted out, but with grands it must be removable so that action and key-frame can be slid out forwards. The key-blocks of the upright occupy space taken up by the pedal connecting rods and frame behind. In grands the treble key-block has an adjustable stop and a locating place for a pin from the key-frame, since this moves to the right when the soft pedal is used. Grand key-blocks are almost always held in place against the cheeks by large bolts or screws under the keybed. Uprights' key-blocks may be screwed in behind the nameboard or obliquely, below the level of the keys so that some keys must be removed before the key-blocks. (*See* Fig. 14).

The various lids are not so called on pianos. As we have seen, that over the keys is called 'the fall'. The principal covers are known as the 'top', that of the grand having front and back halves hinged to each other. Until about 1915 it was general for the back half to be secured by a 'rose' or 'turn-buckle' catch in the bent rim, but this has since become less common – the top is always taken off completely if the piano is to be moved, anyway, so the catch has limited use. There may be long and short props for the top, which tends to be removed for concert performance but has a marked directional acoustic reflecting effect if left in place and open. Upright tops show considerable variety, some opening at the front and some at the right hand side (more like a grand top). In older uprights the back half of the top over the wrestplank is fixed and hinged to the front half which opens. There are many forms of props and stays, as there are of catches for holding the front panel to the sides. Often the latter are badly positioned or insubstantial and cause disagreeable vibrations. Ideally, pianos should be played with the top open, but of course there are many reasons why this is often not done; in particular, playing with the top shut can seem agreeably mellow if in fact the hammers are overdue for toning and the sound seems too bright with the top open.

On uprights the bottom panel beneath the key-bed – sometimes known as the 'bottom door' – normally locates in the 'toe-rail' (a front edge to the bottom board) with dowels or against metal plates, and it is secured by springs or wooden struts or swivels which allow it to open when turned or raised. This panel is a common source of unwanted vibration. In older pianos

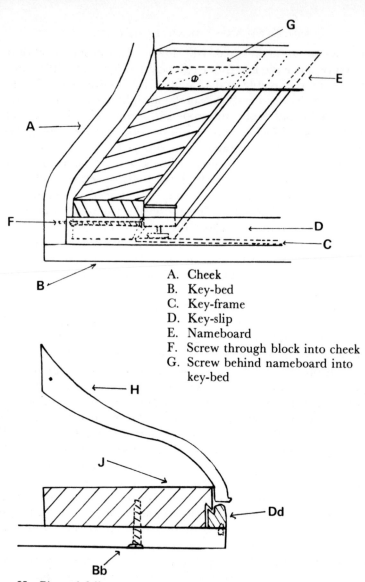

A. Cheek
B. Key-bed
C. Key-frame
D. Key-slip
E. Nameboard
F. Screw through block into cheek
G. Screw behind nameboard into key-bed

H. Pivoted fall
Dd. Key-slip, notched and held by key-block, Located by dowels
J. Key-block, notched to hold key-slip
Bb. Key-bed with screw securing key-bed

Fig. 14. Upright and grand key-blocks

recessed pieces of plywood were often used to give a panelled effect to the top and bottom doors. These frequently shake loose and vibrate when notes of particular pitches are sounded.

Pedals

The sustaining pedals of grands and uprights are similar in that they raise all the dampers simultaneously, whereas the soft pedals of most grands and uprights differ fundamentally in principle and in effect. The upright's soft pedal merely moves all the hammers forwards so that the maximum velocity possible is reduced. This is known as the 'half-blow' action. The grand soft pedal moves the action and key-frame towards the treble so that fewer strings are struck for one note (save, of course, where there is only one string to the note anyway). This is known as 'shift' action. Opinions differ as to which type of action is preferable. The 'shift' introduces a change of tone, partly because fewer strings are struck and partly because a different surface of the hammer may come into use. If the hammer is worn, this difference will be exaggerated, and indeed the system inclines to produce uneven hammer wear. On the other hand, the half-blow action does mechanically what the fingers themselves can do by touch, if less regularly, and also introduces looseness ('lost motion') in the keys, which cease to drive the hammers for the first part of their descent. The tendency to noise and the moving of the keyboard are further demerits of the shift action, but my own feeling is that the whole new scale of tonal variation which it opens up makes it the better system provided that it is well adjusted. There are rare exceptions but by and large the shift system will be found only on grands and the half-blow system only on uprights.

Pedals of uprights used to be pivoted below the bottom board, their rising screws passing up through the board. Nowadays they are mounted inside the case behind the toe-rail. Either way they are linked by rocking arms to respective vertical rods at the side (or at either side) of the case. The pedals are of course depressed, but the mechanism of both requires an upward action, so the rockers are mounted half way along in wooden blocks with pivot pins and by this means the motion of the pedals is inverted. Sometimes coiled springs are used, sometimes bent leaf springs; the latter may themselves serve

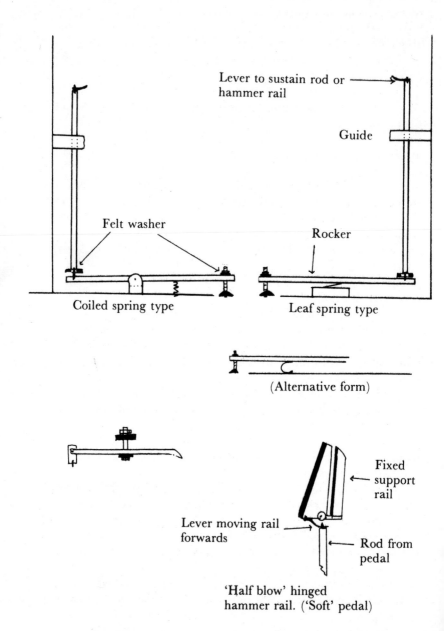

Lever to sustain rod or hammer rail

Guide

Felt washer

Rocker

Coiled spring type

Leaf spring type

(Alternative form)

Lever moving rail forwards

Fixed support rail

Rod from pedal

'Half blow' hinged hammer rail. ('Soft' pedal)

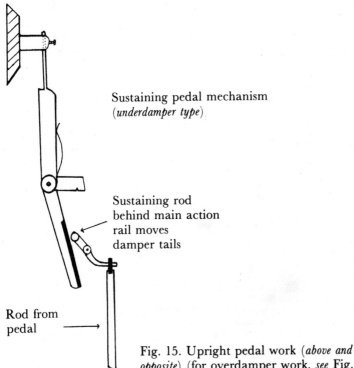

Sustaining pedal mechanism
(*underdamper type*)

Sustaining rod
behind main action
rail moves
damper tails

Rod from
pedal ⟶

Fig. 15. Upright pedal work (*above and opposite*) (for overdamper work, *see* Fig. 31)

as pivots, being attached to rocker and bottom board. The system will be clear from observation (Fig. 15).

The working of grand pedals is less observable. The basic difference is that here the pedals themselves are pivoted midway in the hollowed base of the 'lyre' (nowadays with straight tapered columns), whose top is screwed below the key-bed, and of which one or two rods go back at an angle and are merely supports. Thus the motion at the back end of the pedals is already a rising one and a further rocking connection is not needed. The back ends of the pedals have metal connecting rods resting on their leather pads. The sustaining pedal raises the damper lift rail (in the piano, concealed behind the keys) by means of a wooden link, whilst the soft pedal rod operates an L-shaped crank pivoted in the thickness of the keybed. This catches on the key-frame inside and moves it to the right when the pedal is used. The spring here is a powerful leaf spring in

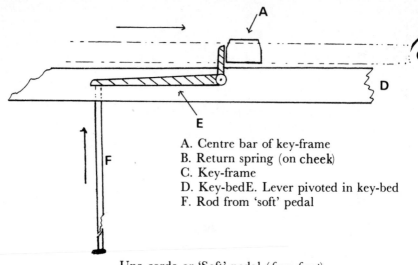

A. Centre bar of key-frame
B. Return spring (on cheek)
C. Key-frame
D. Key-bedE. Lever pivoted in key-bed
F. Rod from 'soft' pedal

Una corda or 'Soft' pedal (*from front*)

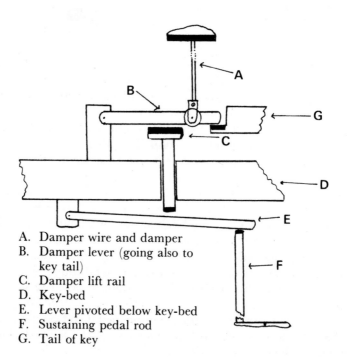

A. Damper wire and damper
B. Damper lever (going also to key tail)
C. Damper lift rail
D. Key-bed
E. Lever pivoted below key-bed
F. Sustaining pedal rod
G. Tail of key

Sustaining pedal (*from side*)

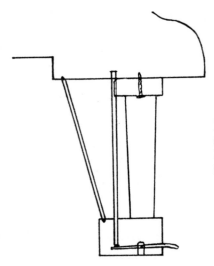

Pedal pivoted mid-way in
short dowel driven into
hollowed block base of lyre.
Support rod to rear

Fig. 16. Grand pedalwork
(*above and opposite*)

the treble cheek, pressing on the key-frame. The sustaining
pedal spring may act directly on the damper lift rail inside or
work on the wooden link which is attached outside and below
the key-bed (*see* Fig. 16).

The purpose of a third pedal varies. Most often in English
and Continental pianos, especially uprights, the middle pedal
by a similar arrangement of rocker and rod operates a 'celeste'
or 'practice' device, which is essentially a strip of cloth inter-
posed between the hammer and the strings. (Sometimes such a
device is operated manually from the top of the case.) Very
occasionally the sustaining work is divided into two parts, so
that the right-hand pedal lifts the upper-note dampers whilst the
middle pedal can be used for separately sustaining the bass. Most
often, in grands, the middle pedal works the 'sostenuto'. When
it is depressed after the note is played, the damper of this note
will be held off the string when the key is released for so long
as the sostenuto pedal is held down. The mechanism and construction are rather complicated, depending on the turning of
a lipped rod to obstruct projecting tabs on such of the damper
levers as are 'up' and to prevent them from falling. This device
has long been favoured on American pianos and appears also
on some Russian and Japanese models, but it has never become

established in Europe generally. It is often felt that the greater tonal power of the bass notes, coupled with the facility to 'half-pedal', are sufficient – the piano, after all, cannot sustain an organ's 'pedal note', whether it has two pedals or three, for the sound is still in constant decay. As a rule notes above the middle cannot be held on half pedal and top notes cannot be sustained independently of lower notes without the third pedal, however. To treat fully of the sostenuto pedal would require disproportionate space here and the reader who is faced with a baffling mechanism should refer to the Bibliography, although generally common sense will see him through.

SOUND-PRODUCING PARTS

This is an ungainly term for several parts of the instrument directly concerned with producing or amplifying vibrations. They are principally the strings (with which we will take the wrestplank and frame) and the soundboard (with which we will take the bridges). The hammers are considered part of the action.

Strings

The vast majority of pianos have 88 notes (variously described as $7\frac{1}{4}$ or $7\frac{1}{3}$ octaves), but some have seven octaves only and relatively few (which are particularly popular in France) have only six octaves; the Bösendorfer Imperial Grand has eight octaves, but we are not likely to be concerned with such an instrument. From the top of the scale down to about Bb an octave below Middle C (i.e. about 63 notes) there are three strings to each note and the strings are of polished steel wire. (Some older economy models had two wire strings to each of these notes.) Each group of three strings is known as a 'trichord'. From then on for an octave or a little more, there are 'bichords' – two strings to a note, the strings being steel wire wound with copper covering. The remaining notes, from nine to thirteen in number, are 'monochords', with single copper-wound strings, there being two copper coverings. Blüthner pianos use in addition a fourth string for each trichord – this is not struck but is tuned to vibrate in sympathy. The exact placing of the breaks between the different stringings varies. Where there are two or three strings to each note, these strings must be finely tuned to each other and each group so tuned is known as a 'unison'. Brushing up the tuning of the unisons often makes a great deal of difference to a piano which is not badly out of tune from note to note.

Modern pianos are 'overstrung' – that is, much of the bass and some tenor stringing (usually, but not always, coinciding with the change from trichords to bichords) passes diagonally above the lower steel stringing. This is partly to save on space – especially in the smallest uprights where overstringing may be extensive – and partly to make the best use of the most resonant area of the soundboard. Overstringing has been used for better-quality pianos since about 1850 and has been virtually universal since about 1930 (Fig. 17). Before this, the strings were laid out in a single solid rank; according to appearance, this is referred to as 'straight', 'parallel', 'oblique' or 'vertical' stringing.

The shortest practicable length of string to produce reasonable tone in the treble is some 55 mm – measured over the part that vibrates (the 'speaking length'), not the total wire. As for a given gauge and density of wire at a certain tension the length is proportional to the frequency, a bottom string of this wire would need to be some 7 m long, which is obviously not feasible. For several reasons it is desirable that the tension on the strings be the same throughout the instrument and therefore a compromise has to be worked, when 'scaling', between lengthening the strings and increasing their mass. In practice this produces the well-known curve of the rim of a grand, observable also inside the upright, together with a carefully graded series of wire gauges down the piano. The gauge changes at least every five notes and, as the wire would be very stiff if appropriately thicker wire were used, steel of much the same gauge as in the lower trichords is used as a core for the copper windings in the bichords and monochords, to increase their mass. Nevertheless, the nearer one can come to the impossible strict relationship of lengths throughout, the better; and, subject to other things, the larger the piano the better.

The covered wire strings are stretched singly between the tuning pin (driven into the wrestplank) and a 'hitchpin' cast in the frame. Generally, each pair of wire strings is a single

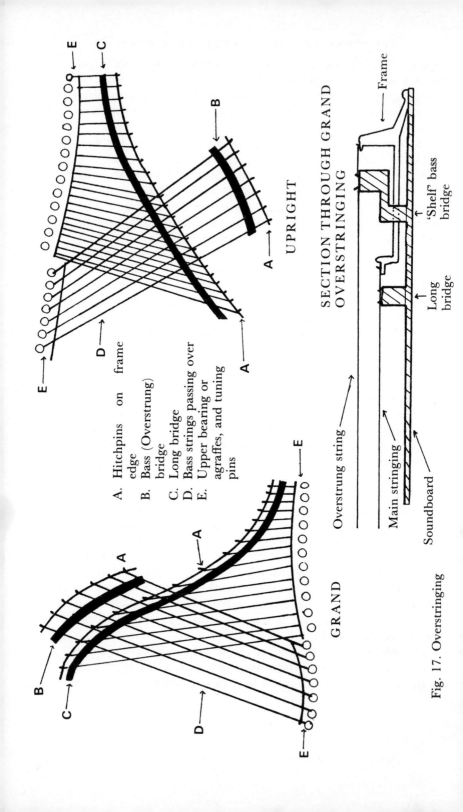

UPRIGHT

A. Hitchpins on frame edge
B. Bass (Overstrung) bridge
C. Long bridge
D. Bass strings passing over
E. Upper bearing or agraffes, and tuning pins

GRAND

SECTION THROUGH GRAND OVERSTRINGING

Frame

Overstrung string

Main stringing

Soundboard

'Shelf' bass bridge

Long bridge

Fig. 17. Overstringing

length of wire bent round a hitchpin and returned to the next wrestpin, although Bösendorfer and Blüthner continue the old method of using single wires throughout, with an eye at each hitchpin. In the normal method it might be thought that tuning one string would affect its other 'half'; in practice because of the friction and stiffness of the wire there is little interference. The 'loop' stringing does, however, mean that the choice of wire gauge is restricted since the wires for a unison should be of the same size and in each pair of trichords there is a wire left over with which to start the next one (Fig. 18). Sometimes manufacturers use an odd single length of wire with an eye to the hitchpin to complete a trichord and to avoid this problem at some stage in the scale; if you are restringing a piano you should take note of where this has been done and restring in the same way.

The 'speaking length' of the strings is between the bridge (on the soundboard) and some edge near the wrestpins. This edge may be a raised bar with another bar ('pressure bar') holding the strings down, or a series of 'studs' (also known as 'agraffes') through which holes in which the wires pass, or a heavy bar ('capo d'astro' bar), part of a grand's frame, below and against which the strings run. By one of these means the strings are forced into a carefully angled path which is critical to tone – down from the wrestplank under the bearing or stud and slightly up towards the edge of the bridge, on to which they must press ('downbearing') if their vibrations are to be conveyed into it and so into the soundboard (Fig. 19). The dead lengths of the strings are usually muted with interwoven braid. Although it is doubtful whether they have perceptible effect, attempts have been made to arrange that the dead lengths are proportionately related to the speaking lengths, and to put them to positive use in other ways.

The tensions now used are very high – say 170 lb per string – and a great strain is placed upon the tuning pins, which must yet not bind in the plank or the instrument will be hard to tune. In fact, well over an inch (at least 30 mm) of pin (and often much more) is driven into the plank at an angle slightly opposite to the direction of strain. The plank itself is drilled with extreme precision to this angle and is secured to both frame and back (though in old uprights the frame may not extend to the plank and in grands only the frame supports the middle

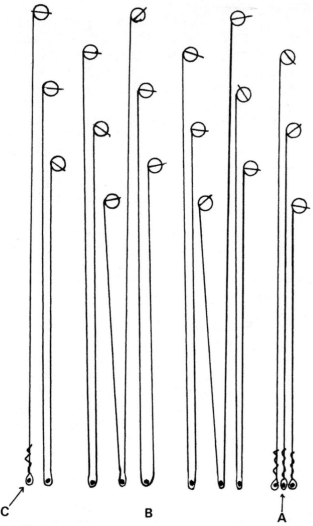

C   B   A

A. Single stringing
B. Loop stringing
C. Here there must be a single string if the gauge of wire is to be changed. Otherwise a trichord would contain wires of mixed gauges

Fig. 18. Loop and single stringing

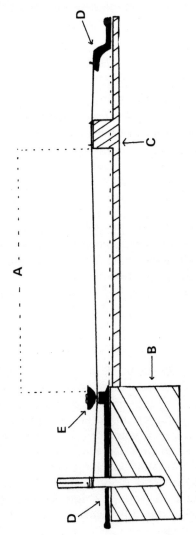

A. Speaking length
B. Wrestplank
C. Soundboard and bridge
D. Frame
E. Pressure bar and upper bearing (or agraffe)

Fig. 19. The path of a string (upright)

of the plank). Wrestplanks are made of hardwood, beech or maple, laminated with the grain in opposite directions. A split or worn-out wrestplank is one of the more serious conditions of old pianos and not easy to detect on a brief inspection since the plank is concealed and the piano may appear to be in tune.

Frame

The other recipient of string tension is the frame. Although experiments have been made with other materials, cast iron is and always has been the normal material for a piano frame since it was introduced in the mid-19th Century. Prior to this, and indeed subsequently, the tension was sustained by wood, sometimes with iron bracings of various sorts, but if there is any intention to have a piano tuned to modern pitch an iron frame is essential. Furthermore, modern heating (primarily because of the dry conditions going with it) is so unsympathetic to timber that it is folly to buy a wooden-framed piano unless it is required for some special purpose and can be carefully cosseted. The iron frame is the heaviest part of the piano and also very vulnerable to shock. It is wise to use at least two people to move a piano frame. This avoids risk of injury to the person, to the frame, and to the soundboard and bridges directly below the frame (below – for the upright must be on its back for this job). A piano with a cracked frame (usually by one of the bars close to the tuning pins) is best avoided; there is very little chance of having the casting repaired or of justifying the expense of trying to do so. The bars referred to are of course structural girders. They have the disadvantage that they usually involve a more or less complete break in the bridges and stringing and, as one such break coincides with the 'break' before the overstringing, it can produce a marked change in tone. However, it is only seldom that bars have been dispensed with and by careful design the break is not usually very noticeable. The frame is mounted on wooden shims or dowels by which its exact height (and so the important 'downbearing' of the strings on the bridges) is set.

Soundboard and Bridges

The purpose of the bridges is to transmit the vibrations to the soundboard. Considered simply, the purpose of the soundboard is to amplify those vibrations so that the compressions and rarefactions of air to be picked up by the listening ear are correspondingly greater. But the soundboard does not simply amplify. Amplification means bringing in some additional energy, which plainly the soundboard does not do. Therefore the apparent amplification must be accomplished with some corresponding loss. What is lost is principally duration; the string would sound for a great deal longer if it did not have to make the soundboard vibrate as well. Equally, the better the piano, the less is lost in this transformation. Secondly, the soundboard distributes the vibrations over a wide area over a period and in the process vibrations from other strings are added, either because the notes are struck or because the dampers are raised. Thus the soundboard is a sensitive store of all the many vibrations at a given moment, some of which were initiated before those of the string most recently struck.

So that vibrations can be transmitted as quickly as possible, all over rather than in only a linear manner, the soundboard is made of planks closely glued (formerly sometimes tongued, but modern glues make this unnecessary) side by side, with the grain running in one direction, and crossed by raised ribs running in the other direction. These ribs also strengthen the board and assist in giving it a slightly domed profile. The dome amounts to about 5 mm, and only 2–3 mm when the strings are on. Many materials have been tried, but, for speed of transmission coupled with reasonable strength, spruce still has the preference. The soundboard is tightly sealed with a hardwood rim where possible, and the tapered ends of the ribs or bars are glued into the sides of the case or back beams. Every effort is made for the soundboard to be a sensitive membrane spreading, without distortion of its own, and according to their original amplitude, the fundamental and partial vibrations of the strings themselves.

In both straight strung and overstrung pianos there are two bridges, the 'long bridge' (which takes care of the trichords) and the 'bass bridge' ('overstrung bridge,' 'short bridge' and other names) which handles the lower notes (Fig. 20). With the straight strung piano these bridges run in the same general direction although the bass bridge has an angle to the long bridge. In overstrung pianos, of course, the bass bridge comes

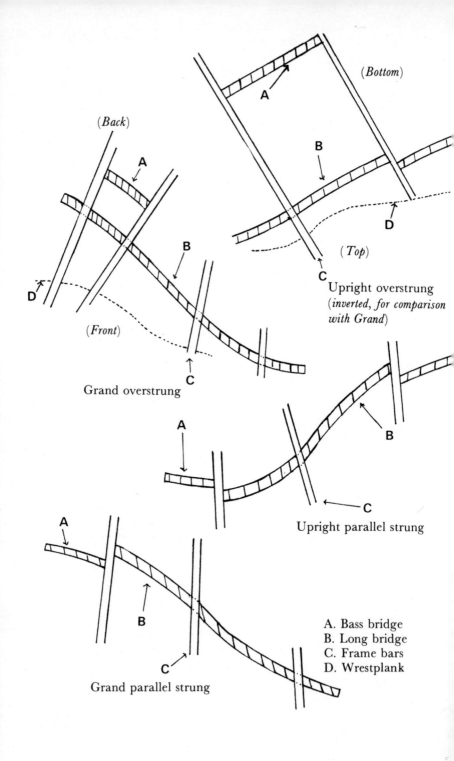

(Bottom)

A

B

D

C (Top)

Upright overstrung
(*inverted, for comparison with Grand*)

(Back)

A

B

D

(Front)

C

Grand overstrung

A

B

C

Upright parallel strung

A

B

C

Grand parallel strung

A. Bass bridge
B. Long bridge
C. Frame bars
D. Wrestplank

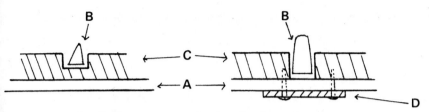

Bridge cut out or broken for frame bars

A. Soundboard
B. Frame bar
C. Bridge
D. Bridging splint below soundboard

Fig. 20. Bridges and frame bars (*above and opposite*)

behind or below part of the long bridge and is higher, so that
the trichord strings can continue beneath it to the bottom part
of the long bridge. It is common for the long bridge to be
divided into two or even three parts to allow passage for bars
in the frame. The bass bridge may be made overhanging as
a shelf with the pins at the outside so that long strings can be
used and yet the bridge not be fixed near the less effective edge
of the soundboard (*see* Fig. 17).

Bridges are made of beech, or sometimes of another hardwood with a beech capping to receive the pins which are likely
to cause splitting if inferior wood is used. The bridges (together
with the pressure bar or agraffes) determine the speaking length
of the strings and their caps are therefore carefully shaped, with
chiselled cut-outs in the line of the bridge pins, to define these
lengths as closely as possible to the design. They are screwed
and glued to the soundboard, the heads of the screws being
recessed in countersunk hardwood 'buttons' which are clearly
visible from under or behind the piano. The shape of the underside of the bridges is exactly matched to the soundboard dome.
Where there is a 'break' there may be a total gap in the bridge,
in which case a piece of hardwood is often placed at that point
behind the soundboard so that in effect the bridge is continued
below. Preferably, there is not a complete break, the bridge

being rebated deeply but not entirely broken to receive the frame bar at that point. The best pianos have indeed not even a rebate, their bars passing over unbroken bridges. At no point may the bridge touch the frame bar, and the soundboard itself is insulated from the frame save at mounting points round the rim. Any central support bolt from the back to the frame clears the soundboard through a large hole.

So that the strings can transmit through the bridges to the soundboard, they must be held on to the bridge – particularly in a grand where the hammer blow is such as to push them away. This is secured first by 'downbearing' (as we have seen). This can be assessed from the angle imposed on the string by the agraffe or pressure bar and hitchpin – or, put another way, by the height of the bridge (though too high a bridge is a poor transmitter). Secondly, the string is held by the 'sidebearing' of the bridge pins, which are driven in at an angle of 70° and staggered so that the string is forced against them by its tension. The firmer the pinning can be the better. Pins are driven about 15 mm into the bridges and there would seem to be some truth in the observation that the better the general quality of the piano, the thicker its bridge pins are.

REPAIRS

Structure

Defects in the back are rare, which is fortunate because, whilst curing them is a matter of common sense and simple carpentry with wood glue and screws, it is likely to involve removing the frame. If you do have to take out the frame, always first take an exact measurement of its height over the soundboard at various points round the edge, and measure the downbearing with your 'E'-gauge and feeler gauges. Removing the frame is naturally a major task since it involves first taking off all the strings (*see* Strings, *below*). The one structural repair which is often required is to the bottom of uprights. Here the bottom board, and often the toe-rail as well, can come away from the sides, especially if the corner toe-blocks are inadequate. This of course makes the piano dangerously unstable as well as creating peculiar noises and rendering pedal action capricious and creaky. To attend to it, you must have the piano on its back. It cannot be overstressed that this is a two-person job – it is essential that someone stands in front to prevent the piano running away as it is tipped, and two people may be needed to take the weight as it goes over. It is also advisable to place a thick board or plank where the top of the back will be on the ground, for without this there can be difficulty in picking it up afterwards without damaging the casework.

The precise repair depends on what is amiss. With older pianos the bottom board comes away from the toe-blocks and can be screwed and glued internally, with additional blocks or angle-irons if necessary. With more modern instruments it is commoner for the toe-blocks or corner battens to come away from the sides. In this case you have to cut an inch of veneer off the bottom, having softened the glue with an iron and damp cloth, so that countersunk screws can be inserted from the outside and then the veneer replaced over them. As a rule it is little use screwing into the sides from within, since they are usually chipboard or blockboard and will not hold the screws adequately, whilst the bottom board is wood and will hold them. On an old piano it is sometimes necessary to reinforce the bottom board with stout battens or to replace it with new timber. Whilst you have the piano on its back, attend to the security of the pedal pivot if it is mounted below the bottom board – you can tighten and lubricate it (with grease) only with the piano lying down.

Whilst the structure is accessible, check the fastness of the wrestplank. It should be solidly glued and screwed to the back and should fit flush. If it is loose enough to remove, have it off and smear it with an even layer of resin filler before replacing it; this will ensure that it fits closely to the back. In the process of getting at these defects you will have had to remove the key-bed bodily, together with the columns if there are any, and now is the time to check their fit. Access to the columns is usually by removing the castors, which will reveal the column screws underneath. The top fastening will probably be by oblique screws through cheeks or key-bed. Insecure castors are dangerous as well as inconvenient. Take the opportunity to fit a new set, preferably of industrial type with nylon or rubber rims. Many old uprights have quite inadequate domestic castors of their period.

71

The weight of grands is better spread and they have fewer structural defects, though these are even more of a problem to reach. Again, simple and massive carpentry is involved, but here you have not only to take off all the strings (*see* Strings, *below*) and extract the frame – which requires three people leaning over the sides, or the use of a hoist and beam – but to turn the whole instrument over. This is heavy work demanding a lot of space; the garage may do, but you will have to protect the finished edges from a concrete floor.

The mounting of the grand wrestplank is inevitably less satisfactory than in uprights. Grand wrestplanks must be firmly screwed to the frame tops and securely lodged in the sides. The same method of making a thin resin bed can be used. There is no room for approximation in fitting a wrestplank for its position governs the course of the stringing. Its holes must align perfectly with those in the frame and no new clearance between plank and frame (or plank and back in an upright) may be introduced, for the height of wrestplank and frame in relation to the soundboard are critical to the tone.

Whilst you have the grand upside down, make good the fitting of the legs and any castors. Strong, freely-moving castors are still more essential with a grand because of the strain taken by the instrument's legs.

The Case

Consider before you attempt work on the case what your limitations are, and what is the value of the piano, real and potential. If you are dealing with a classic 'piano finish' of french polish over selected veneers, it may be wise to have fragments of veneer replaced by a cabinet-maker and the whole professionally polished. This is particularly so of the large surfaces of grands, where it is no easy matter to get a really good french polished finish. On the other hand, if you have an oldish upright, you may care to attempt this work yourself, or you may be happy to strip off the previous finish without damaging the veneer, and to refinish with teak oil or your own less glazed french polishing. A solution of ammonia and soap, given a little time to sink in, will break down any old finish for careful scraping with a scraper and putty knife. The stripped wood needs progressively fine sanding, using a flat cork or wooden block, and then treatment with a grain filler.

Many uprights early this century were finished in black or dark-brown polish or varnish which is opaque and unattractive. The veneer may be found to have a pleasant grain once all this is stripped off, and this patterning will stand out with a fairly simple finish. True ebonizing is a long and complex process outside the scope of most amateurs. Useful instructions are given in Furniglas Information Bulletin No 7 which will enable a reasonable finish with black french polish. A black piano of no special value can be given quite an elegant appearance if rubbed down well and then treated with a mix of blackboard paint and matt polyurethane. A gloss finish on black highlights unevennesses and is generally best avoided by the amateur. Gloss polyurethane and black paint are particularly unattractive. Before deciding what is the appropriate finish, brush up on the subject of wood-finishing from the many books on restoring antique furniture, and experiment on some small surface which can be stripped repeatedly (the key-slip, for instance) rather than starting straight off on the top of a grand or the fall of an upright, which are among the trickier places. Whatever finish you decide to give, remember that in all such work a great part of success lies in proper preparation. You cannot expect to have a reasonable finish on such large flat surfaces unless you spend hours and a great deal of elbow-grease in sanding through reducing grades of paper.

When finishing a case, remove all felt first. Bright new felt does a great deal for appearance; old felt harbours dust. It is best to apply new felt to the finished surface since painting or polishing to the edge is never satisfactory. Consider also at what rubbing surfaces strips of felt may usefully be introduced. It is usual to have three or four felt discs on the underside of the grand top where it contacts the laminated rim. Similarly to prevent vibration, thin felt can often usefully be added round the edges of the top and bottom doors of uprights after making sure that their panels, if fitted, are secure. Always fit new felt – green or red is usual – to the bottom edge of the nameboard, to the backs of grand key-blocks (which stop the fall when it is up for playing), and to the back edge of a grand fall, which acts as a nameboard when the piano is open.

73

Rubber-headed nails can be had in several sizes from good hardware shops. They are useful beneath upright tops (or felt may be used), in the top door or sides where the open fall will rest, and on the key-slip (just in front of the key-blocks) in both uprights and grands, to provide a cushion for the fall. You will not be able to knock them in straight with a hammer and will damage case or nail-head if you try to do so; drill a hole for the nail almost to its full depth, then just tap the nail in.

Fittings

You are unlikely to meet candlesticks on a grand, but they are not uncommon on old uprights and you will have to decide whether or not to keep them. If you do keep them, remove them and soak them in a warm solution of soap (e.g. washing-up liquid) and ammonia to remove old lacquer and tarnish, clean them further with a brass scratch-brush and then polish with any metal polish. If the ammonia solution is unsuccessful, try cellulose thinners on the lacquer. When cleaned, they need to be lacquered to preserve their brightness. You can brush on clear lacquer or spray with an aerosol clear cellulose lacquer obtainable from car shops. The cellulose gives a hard, bright finish. If you require a duller, rather indefinite metallic finish, Hammerite bronze serves well. In theory you can remove candlesticks and plug the screw-holes. In practice this often looks a mess and one would rather have candlesticks, because the wood beneath them will be a different colour from the rest and very hard to tone in. If you are stripping the piano, well and good; you strip the panel and plug the holes with filler, or preferably dowel (filler will show in most finishes). If you are not, you can strip the panels and have them a contrasting colour, or replace them. Best of all, make up a whole new top door from veneered ply or blockboard and choose what finish you wish. This will also obviate the problem of vibrating panels, but it will make the piano an anachronism.

All other brass fittings require similar treatment to that given to retained candlesticks. It makes a tremendous difference to the appearance of even a jaded instrument if the complete hinge and its screws have been removed and polished, and the same applies to the visible parts of locks and to the rim or escutcheon of a lock (which can be dug out and tapped back in). The opportunity should also be taken to tighten up various catches, particularly those between sides and top doors of uprights.

There can be a special nuisance with loose hinges and other parts particularly in modern pianos. Where the screws will not hold in wood fibre, drill out the holes and glue in suitably sized rawplugs before fitting the screws. Grand hinges normally have removable pins so that the tops can be completely removed without difficulty. The holes and pins should be cleaned and thinly greased. These hinges take a great weight and often work loose, damaging the wood around. The appearance is not greatly spoiled if hinges are bolted on, rather than screwed, in such a case. The use of large washers on to the wood spreads the strain.

You have to decide whether to overhaul or to replace an overhanging upright music desk. The swinging slats are usually riveted in place and are best separated for stripping and polishing. File off the rivets and punch them out. The hinges and music clips need to be brightened and the tips of the desk, which rest on the fall when it is open, should have fresh felt pads glued to them and trimmed. There is a lot of work in all this and you may prefer to replace this type with a more modern desk, of which the slip hinged to the underside of the fall is easiest to make. If there is no room for clips, rubber-headed nails cut short can be used instead. If required, clips can be made from brass rod, filed and bent to shape, the ends tapped 4 BA and screwed into slightly under-sized holes. The grand desk and its grooves are likely to need refelting. If the felt has worn away, the wood of both groove and runner may well be damaged so that wear will worsen. The grooves in the desk must be sanded absolutely smooth and then, to secure a reasonably firm fit, the runners (usually screwed into the cheeks) may have to be replaced by hardwood carefully shaped to the new size. Clips are often not fitted to grands, because they can damage the underside of the top. It is possible to fit clips in a felt-covered strip of wood which will rest in place on the desk and serve the same purpose.

Pedals

The simple mechanics (not the regulation, which we will consider below with the Action) of pedals cause a remarkable amount of trouble, especially in uprights. This arises primarily because they and their rockers are pivoted, and therefore move through a circular path, whereas the motion applied and required is vertical (Fig. 15). For example, the 'pedal' end of a rocker describes sideways a circle based on its pivot block on the bottom board, and it rides on the end of the screw fixed to the pedal itself, which is describing a circle from front to back. We do not want a sloppy fitting here, but equally something must give or there will be creaks galore.

The pedal screw should have a leather washer between its head and the underside of the pedal and, if it is the old type passing up through the bottom board, the hole and the pedal pivot must be so adjusted that the screw cannot possibly rub the board – these pivots usually have a sideways adjustment device built in. The screw must move freely in the rocker hole, which can be lubricated with grease and graphite, and there should be a thick felt washer between the top of the rocker and the nut on the screw. (In fact, it is worth inserting a big metal washer between nut and felt as well.) The pedal pivot should be greased. Make quite sure that the wooden cradle in which the rocker pivots is both glued and screwed to the bottom board. These cradles often come loose but remain attached by their screws, and the slightest movement here creates noise. If there is wear, make a new felt or cloth bush in the rocker and cradle. Ensure that the pivot pin is a tight fit – it should be hard to push in unless greased and warm.

If there is a coiled spring, it should locate on hard felt or leather on the rocker, and it is best if a recess is drilled in the bottom board to keep it in place. The hole should be of such a size that the spring has to be pressed in and will stand upright. If there is some form of leaf spring, have it securely fastened at both ends. These springs cannot usually be replaced to size, but it is not difficult to make up a cradle and pivot and to use a coiled spring if a leaf spring is broken or breaking.

The arrangements for vertical rods vary in detail. Generally there is a wooden bracket fixed to the side of the case. This bracket has a felt-bushed hole in it to guide the wood and the felt needs to be in good condition if noise is to be avoided. Rocker and rod end in a pin or a hole – usually the pin is in the rod and the rocker has the hole. Either way, there should

76

be a thick felt washer round the pin so that rocker and rod do not contact wood to wood. The top ends of the vertical rods normally end in pins and these again require felt washers unless the corresponding cranks in the action have rubber grommets or other deadening materials where the rod enters or presses. All these pins on rockers and rods have to be free from rust, and smooth; polish them with very fine emery and metal polish. Do not lubricate them, save with graphite.

Check that the support rods of the grand lyre do support the lyre, which takes great strain in use and is also exposed to accidents. Often the rods are found in effect to have become short. Then you must replace the rod with a longer one, or partially fill up the locating hole. It should not be possible to slide the support rod to and fro once the lyre is screwed home. A lyre which is well screwed at the top – and these arrangements tend to be pretty massive – but not properly supported by the rod will eventually break at the glued joints top and bottom. It must then be dismantled and rebuilt.

Access to the inside of the lyre, and so to the pedals, may be from in front or from underneath. Most often the pedals are pivoted in hard dowels which slot into the hollowed base (Fig. 16). There should be a leather washer between each side of a pedal and its dowel, and the back of the pedal should have a hard leather block on which the pedal rod rests. If the dowels are loose in their sockets, or the pivots are loose in the dowels, the dowels require replacement, for which hardwood dowel must be used. Smear the pivots with grease and graphite but do not lubricate the dowels – you want them firm in the base. The tops of grand pedal rods commonly terminate in threaded sections on which run long capped nuts; these are of course for regulating the pedals and they should have leather or felt buffers where they meet their respective parts in the key-bed. The grand key-frame often has adjustable glides for setting it level and smoothing its movement against the key-bed when the soft pedal is depressed. The key-bed does eventually wear. It must then be finely sanded and thinly rubbed with graphite grease, after which the glides will need adjustment.

Strings

When a single string breaks it does not as a rule do any harm

77

to the frame and remaining stringing. Equally, you may for various reasons remove a single string without risk, although the strings in that vicinity will need to be retuned. Removing a section of strings or all the strings is another matter, however, for unless it is deliberately managed it will subject the frame and soundboard to varying tensions which can cause damage. For this reason it is essential to let strings down gradually rather than in one go, and to do so as far as possible in such a way as to keep the tension constant.

Before you take off any strings, measure the height of the pressure bar (if any) above the frame, because it must be returned similarly. When removing a pressure bar it is best to undo the screws from the two outer ends and work to end in the middle. If, as will occasionally happen, a screw-head breaks off, you will have to drill the screw out or else to drill it and then to use a screw-extractor in it. Either way, mark the hole so that the new screw goes into the right place.

In removing strings, a safe plan is to start in the middle, with the lowest trichords, and to let down one string of each trichord, then to let down one of each bichord and every other mono-chord. Let them down by about one turn of the tuning lever. Then let down the other strings, proceeding alternately. The whole object is to avoid any sudden dropping of tension in a particular area. Then you can start removing the overstrung strings, followed by the steels. Arrange to hang the eyes of the covered strings in order on a length of wire. Similarly, hang the steels, for example on tacks in a shelf, in order, or make micrometer measurements of them and a full list as you take them off if you intend throwing them out and replacing them. Do not remove the tuning pins unless this area needs attention (*see below*). Whilst the wrestplank may be marked with wire gauges, you may not be replacing with the same gauges (there have been several standards), although you must have as nearly as possible the same thickness of wire. If you are going to re-use the same strings it is a mistake to uncoil them at the pin end more than can be avoided; when the tension is off, turn them until you can lever the ends out of the pins and lever the coils off fairly intact but loose. [This is not possible where there are studs (agraffes) for the wire to be taken through.] It is poss-ible to cut the strings off if you are going to replace them, but this is not recommended initially because of the chance that there may be tension left on some strings.

One's first experience of a string breaking during tuning can be rather alarming, but one soon finds that it is not a disaster and that it is a very rare occurrence, though commoner on pianos long neglected and whose wires have set or rusted at the pin. It is here, at this bend or 'becket' that the great majority of breaks occur since, obviously, the outside of the wire is stretched and the inside is compressed as it bends to enter the pin hole. In such a case, if isolated, the same string can be used again with a shorter coil, but this is not ideally desirable and the probability is that the whole wire is fatigued anyway. The other common site for breakage is the stud or bearing bar, for similar reasons.

New covered strings are expensive and may be difficult to obtain. If you order a new string give the supplier too much rather than too little information – send the old string, give make and model if you know them, specify note and octave, send a neighbouring string if a string is missing; a unison string is of course a perfect match and the string either side of a mono-chord will be a very good guide. Failing a source, the broken string can usually be spliced with a short new wire in a certain way (Fig. 21). This is not easy with springy wire and you may find a vice useful as well as pliers and gloves; take your time in coaxing the wire and try not to make any kinks. The join, though not beautiful, will be in the dead length of a stiff string and have little effect on tone, although the string will require a great deal of tuning over a period before it settles down. If these covered strings are thoroughly dirty and sound dull and lumpy, matters can be improved by pulling them through fine emery paper, soaking them in paraffin and brushing them out with a wire brush. When putting them back, turn them at least one full turn in the direction of the winding as they are put in; insert the end through the stud (if any) and tuning pin and wind on some two turns until the eye is nearly level with the hitchpin. Make sure that the string is correctly on the bridge, and then twist the eye round and hold it on to the hitchpin whilst the wrestpin is tightened. It is not a bad idea always to give covered strings this twist, which ensures that core and winding are thoroughly in contact.

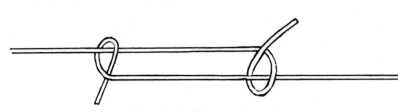

Fig. 21. Splicing strings

For replacing a single string an upright's pressure bar need not be removed and is best left alone. A grand string can be replaced without dismantling the piano. In an upright this may be possible for one string, but it may be necessary to remove the key-bed and this becomes inevitable if one undertakes restringing. As to whether restringing is likely to be worthwhile, there is no simple way of telling. Restringing is lengthy, but the material is not expensive for the improvement which it can give. If there is rust on the steels, if you know that a string has broken or that more than one have done so, or if you have the piano in parts for general reconditioning, then restringing makes sense, and the older the piano the better sense it makes, because there are other factors like a sunken soundboard which you cannot do much about and you may as well give the instrument the benefit of new strings. The diameters of wire in Music Wire Gauge (12–23 by half-sizes cover the usual range of steels) are given in several of the books listed in the Bibliography. They run from 0.71 to 1.30 mm. Where you cannot obtain polished music wire, good steel piano wire will still be some improvement, although it cannot be scaled so accurately since Standard Wire Gauge has only 5 gauges (22–18 s.w.g.) in the required range. (Note that Music Wire Gauge uses high numbers for thick wire and Standard Wire Gauge uses high numbers for thin wire.)

For restringing, wear leather gloves. It is very hard work on the hands and there is also the desirability of keeping finger grease off the bright metal. If you have had the pins out they must be hammered back in with a stout punch to the same height as when they were removed; drive them in – do not screw them until you fit a string. When driving pins in a grand, you must support the frame and wrestplank from below, which can be done with a car jack and a block of wood (Fig. 22). In stringing work from the treble down, keeping a careful check on the wire sizes. Thread the first end into the pin hole, letting it come to the far edge but not beyond and, pulling hard on the string, wind on two turns of wire. Take the wire through the stud, or over the bearing, then over the bridge and down to the hitchpin, round which you bend it sharply but without kinks. Return the wire up to the next pin and cut it off, leaving about 7 cm spare for the three coils. Thread in the end as before and turn the pin, checking as you tighten that the string crosses the bridge correctly. When all is well, tighten both pins until the string is as it will look, but without great tension. If necessary, tighten the beckets at the pins and with pliers close the bend at the hitchpin. Then with the coil lever lift and close up the coils on the pins (Fig. 23). The coils should not touch wrestplank or frame. Tap down all the strings at their hitchpins to make sure that they are seated. The covered strings are treated in the same way – save that they are simpler, being single – and starting from the higher (tenor) end.

Any pressure bar has now to be replaced, to the same height as previously measured, and braid similar to that previously used should be woven between the dead lengths. File out any deep troughs made in the pressure bar by previous strings, but do not alter its contour. Screw the bar on gradually and with care; if you start by screwing any screw right down the bar may well break. It is best to start from the middle and work out to the ends, finishing with each end, as this way any bend in the bar is only gently straightened. Do not over-tighten the screws as this only serves to make tuning difficult, but follow your measurement.

81

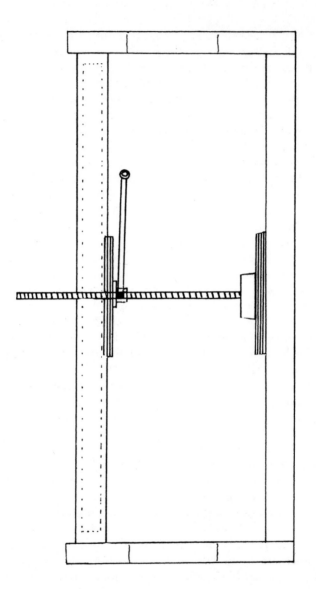

Fig. 22. Supporting the grand wrestplank

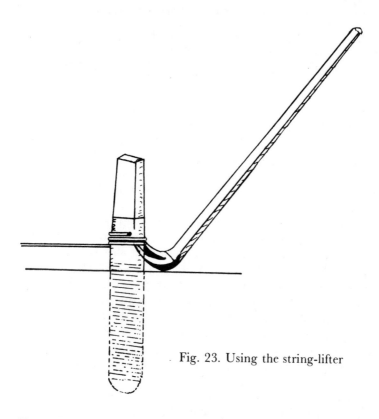

Fig. 23. Using the string-lifter

You have now to restore tension to the strings and frame gradually, and this is done by 'chipping', a rough tuning about an octave below pitch. You can do this against another piano or with a pitch pipe, and indeed you will probably make a reasonable start by ear alone. As the strings are not set, you cannot follow the same procedure as when letting off tension, because at this stage the looped wires will tend to interact with their partners. Instead you have to raise batches of strings throughout the frame – for example, start in the middle and work on alternate treble and bass sides, always tuning complete lengths of wire. Once you have this tension on, you can replace the key-bed of an upright, install the action and line up the strings with the hammer heads using your string-spacer lever. If you are going to work on the action, set the strings with your spacer for you will be able to move the hammers slightly into

83

alignment if necessary. It will require five or six tunings up to proper pitch before the strings will begin to stay in tune and during that time you will not be able to make much of an assessment of the instrument's new tone.

Frame

Soundboard, wrestplank and frame must all be considered together since the distance of the wrestplank and frame from the soundboard is critical to down-bearing and so to tone. If there is no reason to suspect anything amiss, restore plank and frame (whose mounting has been mentioned in 'Structure' above) to the measured height which they had before you dismantled the instrument. On the other hand, you may feel that the soundboard has sunk, and with it the bridges and strings. This may be indicated by a dull tone and almost excessive sustaining when the dampers are up. It is a weary and prolonged thud, if that can be imagined. A sunken soundboard makes the instrument sound round and mature to the point of over-ripeness, when a brighter and clearer tone is wanted – but first make sure that too soft hammer felts are not responsible. When you have the soundboard free of pressure and exposed, place a straight edge right across it; if at the highest point the crown measures much less than 4 mm without the strings it is likely to have sunk. There may also be a detectable dip, seen in the glaze of the varnish, at the long bridge.

There is no way in which the amateur can restore the crown, but there are some ameliorative steps that he can take. One can lower the frame slightly by using thinner shims or washers or lowering the support dowels or bolts of a grand, or otherwise increase down-bearing by changes at the bridge (*see below*) and using thinner felt where the strings rest on the frame. You have, of course, to make no more than one or two millimetres of difference. Some older uprights used hardwood strips on the frame edge, below a felt cover, and these can be minutely reduced, though they must continue to dampen the dead lengths (Fig. 24). Altering the bearing of the dead length will not of itself affect the bearing angle of the crucial speaking length of the string, but it will improve contact with the bridge.

The cushion felts on the frame edges should be removed and replaced in any case. Whilst you have them off, rub down the

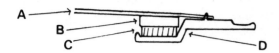

A. String
B. Listing felt
C. Wooden strip
D. Edge of frame

Fig. 24. Hitchpin and edging strip

frame with steel wool, removing all rust (which can spread to the strings). File out any grooves which there may be in the capo d'astro or pressure bar, but remove as little metal as possible and polish the new surfaces with fine emery. Before replacing the felts, spray or paint the frame and pressure bar (avoiding polished surfaces) with bronze or gold paint and follow this with clear lacquer. If there has been heavy rust, it is worth applying a rust killer and zinc primer before painting. Quite often only the top visible parts of uprights frames are painted a metallic colour, the remainder being grey or black.

Remember that the frame is heavy, awkward and very brittle. Be over-cautious in moving it and laying it down, rather than risk a crack or break which cannot be required. In screwing the renovated frame back into the piano, do so gradually, checking the heights and tightening all screws at first only moderately. Do not screw up tightly on one side and then do the same on the other, for this will impose great strain against the normal path of stress. Only when all screws are in and their heads touching the frame, with the frame unable to be tilted any way, is it safe to tighten home the screws.

Wrestplank

The wrestplank is the key to stability of tuning (provided that tuning is properly carried out). The necessary tightness of the pins is best found by experiment and you will soon acquire a feel for it. A rough guide is that at least 5 lb pressure on the torque wrench should be needed to undo a pin with the string on, and about 14 lb to tighten the string by an actual movement of the pin. If you have found one or two pins to be loose, check that the plank is not cracked – though a crack may be invisible behind the frame or back until you dismantle – and then try wedging the pins, driving them in with emery paper bushes, medium grade folded so that the rough side is towards both metal and wood. Slithers from plastic rawlplugs can also be effective – but only slithers, not pieces large enough to deform the holes. Another approach is to remove the offending pins completely and to measure the depth of their holes. You may then drive them in further provided that there is clearance – if there is not, you risk loosening and splitting the block. Do not drive pins in in hopes as the piano stands; at least take the tension off the wire and surrounding strings and make very sure to support the wrestplank of a grand (as mentioned under 'Strings' above). Again, do not put epoxy resin down the holes or you will make tuning impossible.

Where loose pins are general, 'doping' can be effective and may be repeated on occasions. You can buy liquid 'pin-block restorer' or use your own solution of glycerine and methylated spirits. These compositions are hygroscopic – they act by absorbing atmospheric moisture which then swells the surrounding wood. Never let them touch the strings, or the latter will rapidly corrode. A grand can be doped where it stands but an upright must be laid on its back. Use a hypodermic or a medicine dropper and apply one or two drops of the fluid to the junction of pin and wrestplank. Capillary action will draw the mixture round the pin in a circle. More than one application is usually necessary, so you may as well do the job three times in a week before you assess the results. If you have dismantled a piano known to have loose pins, let a little dope into the holes whilst the pins are out and then apply some more when the strings are back on.

If all else fails, you may be able to obtain a set of slightly larger pins from your supplier or from a junk piano dealer. Where the plank does on inspection turn out to be cracked it is worth trying to fill the crack with epoxy resin, but often the crack is in inaccessible laminations within and the only hope lies in a new block, the making and fitting of which is best left to professionals.

Tuning pins must be free of rust. Above ground, rust spreads to the strings and below ground it causes the pins to 'grab', which makes tuning very difficult. If you can, brush the pin on a rotary steel wire brush. Otherwise do what you can with a hand brush and emery. The tops of the pins can be blued or treated with thin matt black paint to protect them. Where they have been mauled, try to hammer the affected metal straight before dressing with a fine file.

When as is now general, a wrestplank is covered by a frame, it requires no finishing. Where it is uncovered, clean it up and apply polyurethane varnish.

Soundboard and Bridges

The soundboard and bridges are critical to tone, but it is not easy to assess or alter them from this point of view and repairs are confined largely to remedying visible defects. A few hairline cracks are of little significance, but any cracking of the sound-board along its joints, any breakdown of the edges, and any looseness of the bars or bridges detrimentally affects tone and must be amended. Uprights are not affected, but grands rapidly accumulate a thick carpet of dust – not to mention pins, paper-clips etc., especially in schools and church halls – which significantly dampens tone and also makes assessment of their condition more difficult. They can be cleaned out by means of a springy metal strip attached to a cloth, long-handled paint-brushes, and anything else you care to try which will avoid your having (at least initially) to remove frame and strings. For this cleaning job it is sensible to remove the action so that it does not receive showers of dust, and to give the key-bed a good clean at the same time. It is also worth remembering that some vacuum cleaners can be reversed to blow rather than to suck.

Most repairs to the soundboard will involve removing the frame and strings, since the whole will have to be refinished. Before removing these parts, take measurements of bearing, the height of the frame above the soundboard and the height of the pressure bar if any. Measure the down-bearing of the speaking length of the string, in relation to the top of the bridge, either in degrees (there should be at least 1°, but this way of measuring is not easy), or in millimetres using your 'E'-gauge and feeler gauge (Fig. 25). These measurements are so that you restore the instrument exactly as it was unless you make deliberate small changes. To try to remove the soundboard is to ask for trouble. If it is insecure at any place, fill the gap with

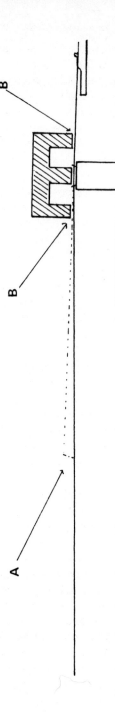

A. Measure with protractor, or
B. Measure with feeler gauge, placing centre of 'E' gauge level on string where it crosses bridge

Fig. 25. Measuring down-bearing

glue and if necessary put in a temporary screw, which can be replaced with glued dowel once the edge has set.

Superficial soundboard cracks can be filled with a woody mixture of sawdust and epoxy resin, pressed well in and sanded level. Deep cracks, particularly between planks, must be filled with glued wooden shims. This may require prior enlargement into a deep 'vee' trench. The shim should be sharp and tight enough to have to be tapped into place. Ideally, it will be of spruce from a supplier, but pine is satisfactory. Such cracks are almost always complex in practice; it is not simply that a gap appears between parallel boards, but that either or both boards warp upwards and come away from the soundboard bars. The loose bar can be detected by placing hand pressure on the soundboard when the instrument is played loudly, and it may audibly buzz. In such a case, before you can do your work with the shims, you must have the boards levelled and firmly glued to their bar or bars. To screw them down is unsightly and in all probability they will split away again leaving a nasty hole into the bargain. Instead, drill holes right through the board and bar to accommodate bolts, say 8 cm long. Inject glue between the bar and the planks and put a big washer on the bolt's head where it goes through the bar. Where the bolts come through the soundboard have a piece of plywood sufficient to spread the strain of this temporary fastening drilled for the bolts, and clamp down the nuts until the glue is well set. When the glue is hard, remove bolts and wood and plug the holes with dowel, which should have channels made along it to hold the glue (Fig. 26). This sort of repair will help to restore the crown, holding the boards to the curved bar, as well as cure looseness.

It is very difficult indeed to remove a bridge without damaging its soundboard. If part of the glueing has failed, try running vinegar into the remainder after unscrewing from behind the soundboard. (Take care not to damage the brittle wooden 'buttons' with your screwdriver.) If the bridge will not come loose, do not persist. Resign yourself to scraping away as much of the broken glue as possible, applying fresh glue and screwing up. The flow of the glue will be helped if you can warm the bridge and affected area of the soundboard, say with a warm (not hot) iron from behind.

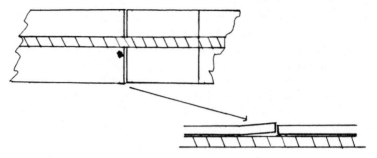

Common complex defect – soundboard crack and warping, with loose soundboard bar

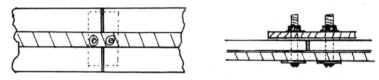

The above under repair using bolts and washers through bar, re-glued, and wood strip to spread strain of flattening warp. Crack may still need filling afterwards. Holes plugged with dowel.

Fig. 26. Repairing soundboard

If you think the soundboard sunken and the downbearing inadequate, and you have the bridge off, cut hardwood veneer of the desired thickness, and glue it to the underside of the bridge, pounding it with a soft-headed hammer (or hammer with soft mask) and leaving a slight edge. Trim off the edge when it is set, apply more glue to this new lower surface of the bridge and screw up tightly to the soundboard. I have been told that it is possible to apply veneer to the top of the bridge, if you do not wish to remove the bridge, but I have not found this satisfactory.

The commonest faults with bridges are loose pins and the breaking up of the top of the bridge because of the strain on the pins. This produces distinct, usually 'ringing', tone in affected notes. Where the breakdown is not general repair work can be done without removing the bridge and consists of taking

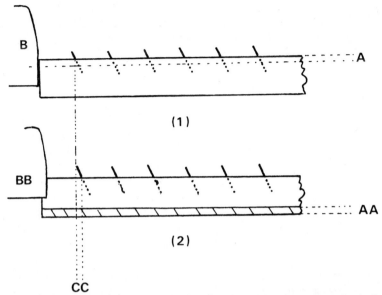

(1)

(2)

In (1) the bridge is badly cracked in the top section A, and closely abutts frame bar B. In (2) a new plinth AA is made to the exact thickness of A, which has been planed off. As the same pin holes are used, the bridge must be moved on the soundboard to the extent shown at CC, and as a result clearance must be cut for the frame at BB.

Fig. 27. Bridge repair

out the pins and filling the holes and cracks with epoxy resin. It is best to heat each pin with a soldering iron to make it easier to remove. Replace the pins before the glue sets, and trim away any raised epoxy resin before it hardens. On no account try to solve a problem by knocking bigger pins into the worn holes, since this will misplace the strings even if you can get them into place between the pins; and do not clout existing pins in further – they will be no firmer at the top, can damage the bridge and will not hold the strings.

If the trouble is more extensive, it is possible to have a new cap for a bridge made or to attempt a repair yourself (Fig. 27). For this you must remove all the pins and plane down the bridge until the pinholes are clean and round. The utmost care is needed to ensure that the bridge is kept both flat and of even height overall, so you must take exact measurements of the bridge before you start. The next job is to make from hardwood, preferably beech or maple, a base of exactly the same thickness as the top surface which has been removed. Its underside has to be sanded until it is a complete fit for the soundboard; you can judge this from the old bottom of the bridge once you have removed all glue so that the new plinth can be fitted without adding to the total height. You want a complete layer of glue, but a very thin one, for this join. The new pins – for which decapitated nails are satisfactory in an ordinary model – must be driven in at an angle of 70°, be sited exactly as before and be of the same thickness as the original pins. As you are using the old holes, deepened, the bridge will have to be very slightly moved to preserve the course of the strings, and may require minor surgery to clear the bars of the frame (Fig. 28). Do not attempt to drive the pins straight in – you will probably break or bend them and in any case the angle will be haphazard. Instead, use a slightly small drill to feel your way down the existing holes and drill to about half the length of the pins before driving them in. When all the pins are fitted, file or stone over their ends until they are flat and parallel to the bridge top – it is a small point which contributes a great deal to appearance. About a third – say 3–4 mm – of the pins' length should be above the bridge in the end. Finally, you have to make a reasonable attempt at a craftsman's job – cutting the bridge edge in front of each group of pins to allow clearance for the string and a definite start to the speaking length. Parts of the original cuts will still be visible, but you will have to bring them back to the new positions of the pins. A fine hacksaw and chisel, which you will have constantly to rehone, are best for this.

The side of bridges and the whole soundboard should be sanded with increasingly fine paper and steel wool (along the grain) and then varnished. Do not varnish the bridge until it is secured to the soundboard – they should look and be as one. There has over the years been some debate as to the best varnish to use. The coating is almost certainly protective from the atmosphere and does not mature to contribute to tone (as does that on a violin, for example). Clear polyurethane is tough and I have not found it detrimental. Whatever you use, take a pride in the sealing and finishing of bridges and soundboard. They are a very visible evidence of your craftsmanship and very satisfying to do well.

It is often customary to paint the tops of bridges with black lead as this is considered to ease the passage of the wires during tuning and indeed it looks well. However, many bridges are not so finished and the choice is yours. It is not easy to clean bridge pins *in situ* effectively and without destroying the appearance and possibly the surface of the bridge top. It is much better to replace the pins. However, if it is decided to clean some, extract them as above, clean them with wire brush and emery, and knock them back with the merest touch of epoxy resin on the bottoms.

Chapter Four

THE UPRIGHT ACTION

Structure

Actions these days are pretty standardized, being bought in by builders from specialist houses, although a few (including some of the most celebrated) builders still make their own actions.

A regular form of action is illustrated in Fig. 28. It comprises iron end-pieces ('standards') and shaped wooden 'rails' to which are screwed the pivoted brackets ('flanges') of wippens, hammers and damper bodies. There may also be several intermediate standards. Some makers use metal rails, and there is an increasing tendency to use some form of plastic (rather than wooden) flange. At the top, the standards screw into the frame and back, either directly or into long adjustable bolts. At the bottom the feet may be domed and fit into bolts with hollow heads in the key-bed, or they may be hooked brackets which locate on to projecting bolts. There may or may not be some means of adjusting the height of the action; this, which determines where the strings are struck, is very critical to tone and there will not normally be any reason to alter the builder's setting. Older upright actions have hardwood ends into which the rails are mortised. These ends rest on wooden blocks in the key-beds and are usually located with dowels. They can be raised or lowered only with difficulty. The tops of the wooden standards have small brass clips which fit into slots in wooden blocks attached to the sides of the case, and so fasten the action into position.

Perhaps the most critical parts of actions are the pivots and bushed holes which together make up a 'centre'. If these are tight, the associated piece is sluggish or jams or is noisy. If they are loose, there is excessive 'travel' in the piece, the proper surfaces do not mate, the hammers do not strike true and the whole performance is unreliable and unpredictable. In each of the many centres in one action the moving part is transfixed by a 'centre pin', formerly of brass, now generally of polished steel,

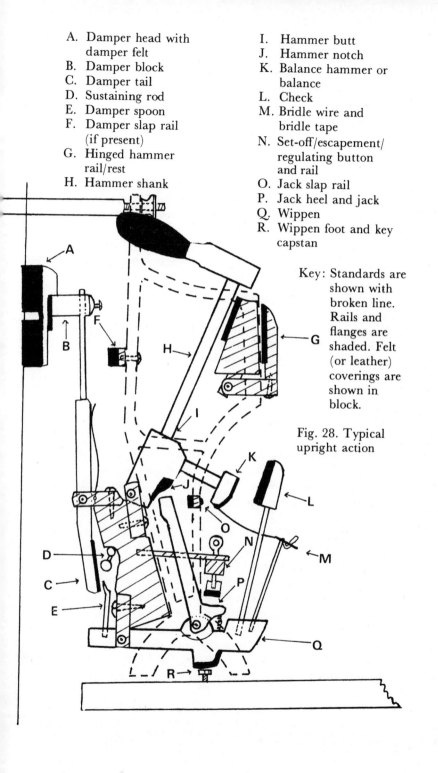

A. Damper head with damper felt
B. Damper block
C. Damper tail
D. Sustaining rod
E. Damper spoon
F. Damper slap rail (if present)
G. Hinged hammer rail/rest
H. Hammer shank
I. Hammer butt
J. Hammer notch
K. Balance hammer or balance
L. Check
M. Bridle wire and bridle tape
N. Set-off/escapement/regulating button and rail
O. Jack slap rail
P. Jack heel and jack
Q. Wippen
R. Wippen foot and key capstan

Key: Standards are shown with broken line. Rails and flanges are shaded. Felt (or leather) coverings are shown in block.

Fig. 28. Typical upright action

which forms the pivot. The pin is (usually) driven in and (always) fixed to the moving part so that it moves with it. Receiving the pin are the static holes of the 'flange'. These are carefully bushed with felt or cloth such that the part has free but accurate movement. Nowadays plastics are being used for flange bushings and will have a longer life (*see* Fig. 29).

The action is built up on a central beam or rail which carries the hammers, wippens and dampers, as well as the cranked sustaining pedal rod sunk into a hollow at the back where it acts on the damper tails. Also attached to the standards is the hammer rail, on which the hammer heads rest at the front. Certain subsidiary rails for limiting the movements of jacks and dampers, and to house the regulating buttons, may be mounted by supports on the main beam or be taken through to the standards.

It will be noticed that once the keys are removed, the wippens will incline to fall downwards with the result that the jacks become displaced from the hammer butts. This, for 88 units, would be inconvenient and is one of the reasons for the 'bridle tapes' connecting hammers and wippens.

Working

The principle of the working has already been outlined in Chapter 1 in connection with touch. Plates 6–9 show the sequence of events in an actual action. Note in particular the relative positions of damper, hammer and jack at each stage. (The action pictured here is from a player piano and this is the reason for an extra felt pad at the wippen front which is not seen in Fig. 29. There is no other difference between the actions.)

To begin with, it is essential that the hammer starts from rest, just touching the hammer rail. If it is raised off the rail before moving, the touch will seem heavy and some power will be lost in that the key will move its full distance (10 mm), but the hammer will not. The 'strike distance' of the hammer from the string is normally 50 mm, as has been noted. Particular makes vary, but that is a good general rule. If the hammer is on the rail and there is more than this distance to the string, repairs will have to be made (*see below*, 'Repairs'). More usually, the basic strike distance is acceptable but the hammer shank is raised

96

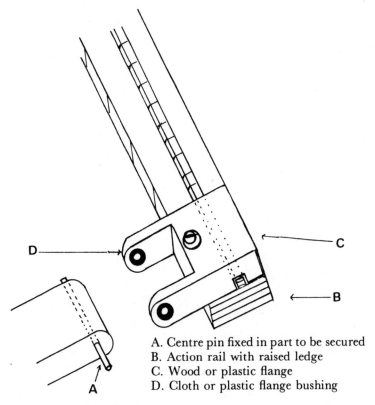

A. Centre pin fixed in part to be secured
B. Action rail with raised ledge
C. Wood or plastic flange
D. Cloth or plastic flange bushing

Fig. 29. Action centre and flange

off the hammer rail. This is corrected by screwing down the key capstans (which vary in form according to date but can always be adjusted). If the capstans are right down already, the action is too low or the key-frame – which is usually raised on shims in the key-bed – is too high. When the hammer is correctly rested, the jack tips should be just below the hammer butt notch. If they are too high, the capstans need lowering, and if too low the capstans need raising (Fig. 30).

All these things must be right if the hammer is to get properly under way. Once the hammer is in motion, the next stage is for the damper to rise (Plate 7). The damper is moved by an upright wire ending in a flat hollow and known as the 'damper spoon'. The spoon is fixed to the wippen and presses against the damper tail as the wippen tilts on its centre under pressure

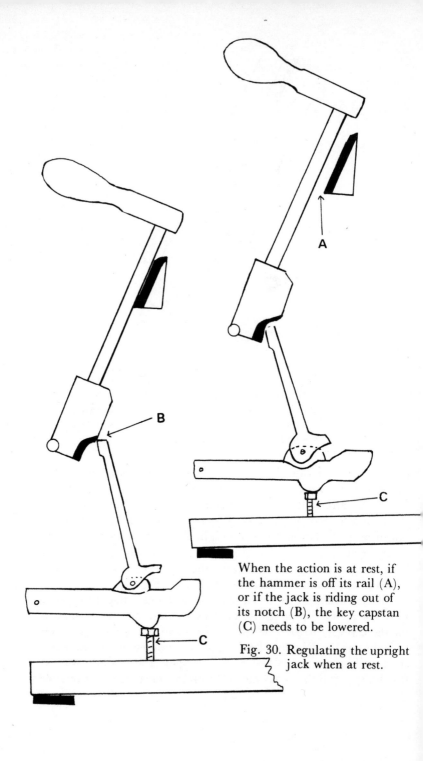

When the action is at rest, if the hammer is off its rail (A), or if the jack is riding out of its notch (B), the key capstan (C) needs to be lowered.

Fig. 30. Regulating the upright jack when at rest.

from the key capstan. The damper should start to move when the hammer is about half-way to the string, or its striking surface is just above the damper's fixing screw. There is some leeway here, which can be used for adjusting touch, but if the damper moves too early there will be blurred notes and if it moves too late it will return early and stifle the full tone. The regulation of this form of damper is not easy and will be considered shortly.

The key now has the weight of hammer and damper (with spring) on it, and it next takes on the final load, that involved in the escapement as the jack tip struggles to come out from the hammer notch under the influence of the increasing pressure of the regulating button ('set-off button') on its heel. This escapement of the jack should occur with the hammer as close to the string as possible, so long as the jack does positively flip away from the notch (Plate 8). This is of course arranged by adjusting the height of the set-off button with its screw.

The hammer, entirely detached from the key, strikes and rebounds from the string and the return phase commences. According to how far down the key may still be, keeping the wippen raised, the hammer's 'balance' or 'back-stop' is caught by the 'check' as the jack heel is released by the set-off button, and the jack's tip thus has an instant in which to resume its position below the hammer butt (Plate 9). The hammer's rapid rebound is assisted first by the hammer spring and secondly by the tautening of the bridle tape as the wippen falls away and the key comes up. Both check and tape have to be carefully adjusted. It will be noted that the key plays no part in this; it is quite possible for the key, by its own balance and the effect of the damper spring, to come back up in advance of the return of the hammer and fall off the wippen, if the centres are sluggish.

Overdamper Actions

This is an 'underdamper' action of the type now universally used; the damper is below, but very close to, the hammer's strike point. Older actions are frequently of the 'overdamper' type, in which the dampers are centred on a rail above the hammers and are operated by wire rods coming up in front of the action from the wippens (*see* Fig. 31). These dampers return

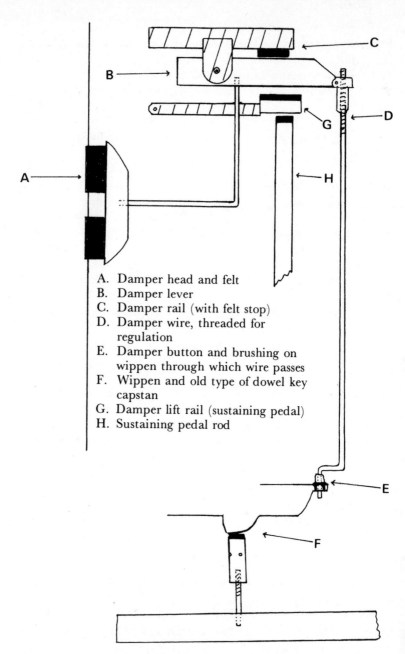

A. Damper head and felt
B. Damper lever
C. Damper rail (with felt stop)
D. Damper wire, threaded for regulation
E. Damper button and brushing on wippen through which wire passes
F. Wippen and old type of dowel key capstan
G. Damper lift rail (sustaining pedal)
H. Sustaining pedal rod

Fig. 31. Overdamper mechanism

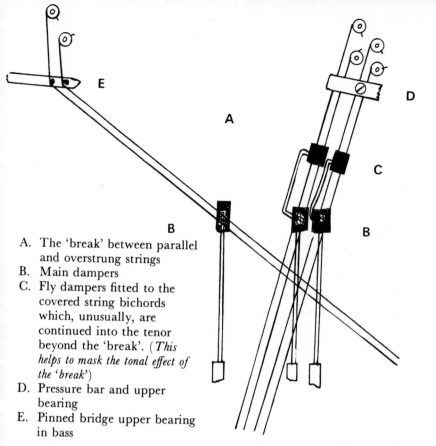

A. The 'break' between parallel and overstrung strings
B. Main dampers
C. Fly dampers fitted to the covered string bichords which, unusually, are continued into the tenor beyond the 'break'. (*This helps to mask the tonal effect of the 'break'*)
D. Pressure bar and upper bearing
E. Pinned bridge upper bearing in bass

Fig. 32. Flydampers

to the string by gravity, not by a spring. (They should not be confused with subsidiary overdampers – known as 'fly dampers' – fitted on some underdamper actions for extra damping of the strings around the bass break – *see* Fig. 32.) The overdamper may seem to have the advantage in that, like grand dampers, it is operated by gravity and has a more consistent effect on touch. It is also a good deal more easy to regulate, although its presence complicates regulating the rest of the action. But these points are outweighed by its greater distance from the point where the string is struck and where the vibrations are best able to be quickly and effectively damped.

For overdampers, disregard what is said below as to removal and regulation of dampers. The overdamper rail is fixed to the wooden standards of the action and the dampers can be dealt with as a separate unit. Remove this before you tackle the rest of the action. When servicing the dampers, number them before you remove them from their flanges, and mark the wires where they enter the top fitting, as a help to regulation later. The replacement of felts is as for underdampers save that the treble dampers are small strips of felt stuck into and protruding from the damper heads and you will have to make up new felts if you replace them. It is common for the weights in these dampers to swell out so that they rub their neighbours, which produces erratic damping. As you go through the dampers tap all their weights flat with the wood – gently so as not to split the wood at this point. When you reassemble the action, these dampers go on and are regulated last, with the action in the piano. To regulate, bend the wires in the dampers themselves, and screw the main damper wires up or down according to whether damping from the keys is early or late – the requirements here are as for underdampers.

REPAIRS

Dismantling

You will have to decide whether to dismantle the action completely or whether to rely on visual and manual checks to detect isolated places needing attention. There is much to be said for doing the complete job; many individual breakages, for example of springs or unglued felts, in fact indicate the need of the whole action for an overhaul, and if you merely repair two or three pieces you will find that the same repair has to be carried out elsewhere within a short time.

Actions, like frames, are heavy and fragile and they need forethought as to their handling. The upright action with metal standards is particularly difficult to support for work when out of the piano, though some old ones will stand on the bench. You can construct a rough jib with a clamp or vice for the purpose, manage by keeping it as far as possible on its front (i.e. with dampers up) with blocks under the standards keeping it clear of bench or table, or you can suspend it from a bracket or hooks screwed to a wall or shelf, the hooks passing beneath the hammer rail or through holes in the standards.

If you dismantle the action completely, follow an orderly procedure. The parts must go back where they came from and they may not be interchangeable. You need a lot of space on which to lay them out in order, and it is sensible to number them in pencil, starting from the bass each time. Often you will find that they have been numbered before or have their numbers stamped on them.

The first thing to do is to remove the tapes from their bridle wires. (Do not do this with the action in the piano or it will fall apart when you take it out, which will complicate the work and increase the risk of damage.) Tapes are most easily removed with stout tweezers or long-nosed pliers and there is a knack in holding up the wippens and twisting the tape tips to remove them from the looped wires. Do not be too delicate, however; if the old leather tips are rotten they must be replaced rather than be left in doubtful condition, and they may as well break now as when you try to put them back. The ends harden and crack at the holes; cracked ends should certainly be replaced. There are various commercial tips of leather and plastic, but you can make quite satisfactory replacements of your own from soft leather fixed with impact adhesive. This can be done now or left till later.

When you have the tapes disconnected, unscrew the wippens and lay them out, being careful not to lose the jack springs. (In some cases there is a spring from the jack connecting with a silk loop from the hammer butt. This must be disconnected before hammer or wippen can be removed.) Then remove the hammers and hammer rail, lay them out and do the same with the dampers and damper rail. Lastly, remove the jack slap rail and set-off button rail. Some actions do not have damper or jack slap rails. Instead of a slap rail, the jack may have a felt button below the tip which is placed to meet a projection on the hammer balance, so limiting the jack's movement.

Centres

With all the moving parts you have to consider the action and condition of the centres, so a general word will be said about this here. Generally tight centres are commoner than loose ones and the latter will be obvious from the sloppy movement of the pins seen end-wise. What you require of a centre is that when the part is held with the loose flange horizontal, the flange (with its screw) will fall smoothly by its own weight towards the vertical. As a rule, the pin is driven into the moving part, but on some upright hammer butts it is held in place by a clamp, a screwed metal plate pressing on the pin. For the hammer to strike true, the pin must be tight in the butt, the ends be just free in the flange bushings. Do not attempt to compensate for tight bushings by leaving the pin loose under its clamp, for this will result in erratic striking by the hammer and the pin will eventually loosen further.

Where a centre is only slightly tight, it may be possible to free it without taking it apart. Apply a minute drop of water to the wood round the bushing, which will shrink it after initial swelling. Alternatively, or afterwards, apply a hot soldering iron to the pin, trying not to scorch the bushing. If these devices fail, you will have to strip down the centre. This involves very carefully driving out the centre pin with a fine straight punch, which will be easier if the pin has previously been heated. Care is needed because action wood is brittle and flanges are delicate and difficult to repair strongly. Once you have the pin removed, trim the inner edges of the bushing with a razor blade if they protrude. Then find a wire which is a slightly tight fit for the flange holes and heat it, well below red heat, and rub it to and fro in the bushings. If the pin was very tight, roughen the wire slightly with a file first. At every stage, test the fit of the pin.

If all is to no avail, or if the bushing is damaged, you will have to renew the bushes. Pry out the old cloth without spoiling the surrounding wood – it may help to let a drop of methylated spirit soak into the bushing first. Use a new centre pin of the same size, or measure it with your micrometer and select a short length of dead straight piano wire of the same gauge. Wrap thin felt or cloth round the pin so that you can cut a strip the width of its circumference – it is better to be slightly too small than to end up with a double thickness through using too wide a strip – and shape the end into a long central point. Push this through one hole, with the cloth hollowed, and then on through the other and pull it a little way with tweezers or pliers. When you have a good cylinder going through both holes, apply a little glue at the entry points and pull the cloth through until the glue is inside. Explore with a finer piano wire to make sure that the walls of the bushing are in contact with the wood, and then leave to dry. When the bushing is dry, cut away between the holes and trim all four sides with a razor blade. It may well be that the new bushing is too tight, in which case you start with loosening methods again. This is fiddly but very important work. Plastic bushings are widely used in modern pianos and are available for standard pin sizes. I have found that selected pieces of PVC insulation from electrical wires make good bushings in an emergency and you may care to try your hand with them. It is easiest to bush holes separately, rather than in pairs, with these improvised bushes.

Action Rails

Renew the felts on the various rails as a matter of course. This is a straightforward and satisfying job. Be careful, however, with the baize on the hammer rail. It will almost certainly be grooved from the pressure of the hammer shanks and you have to estimate its original thickness in order to secure the correct strike distance; you can add thin felt later, though less easily, but you cannot easily reduce felt once it is stuck down. Whilst you have the rail to hand, check its truth against a straight edge. Some actions have a central support, but in any case rails sink down and backwards over the years and this causes unequal strike distances in the scale. If a warp is not large, clamp the rail to a straight board and steam it till thoroughly damp – a kettle will do – then leave it clamped to dry out. If the warp is more serious you may be able to make good by packing the rail felt in the centre, but it is far better to replace the rail with new wood. This should be hardwood if warping is to be restricted in the future. Always make sure that the soft pedal crank is firmly screwed to the hammer rail, whether old or new. To the set-off rail on a rusted old action apply a drop of solvent (e.g. 'Three In One') to each set-off screw where it comes through the rail and then test that all will turn. If they will not, try heating with the soldering iron first. Do not be rough with these screws. A rusty screw is very liable to break off as you attempt to regulate, and it is not easy to remove or replace. At the same time, renew any worn set-off button felts with punched discs. The wooden buttons screw on, and split if over-tightened. Pieces of dowel make satisfactory replacements.

Hammers

You cannot deal properly with the hammer heads until the action is reinstated, so these are considered in Chapter 7; however, if you need to do any re-covering refer to that Chapter now.

You may have noticed warped or broken hammer shanks before taking the action down. Warped shanks can be steamed. Broken ones are better replaced, as no glued or splinted repair is as satisfactory as even an inferior new shank. However, if you have a long clean slit in a shank it can be glued and bound with fine twine, the twine itself then being given a coat of glue. If at all possible, avoid drilling out the old stumps, because it is very difficult to assess the exact angle required, let alone to drill it. Allow a little vinegar to soak in and then see if you can twist the broken shanks out, when you will be able to clean up the holes. If you have no new shank or dowel of the right size, do not enlarge the hole, but reduce the intended shank. Cut a new shank just a little short of the length required, so that the head can be pushed on further if necessary if the hole in the head is blind. Deeply scratch the ends of the shank or roll them under a coarse file (so as to leave room for glue in the joint) and then press the butt end in. It is usual to leave the glue which bubbles up out of the hole. The head can be fitted in the same way but is best left for now, as otherwise you will almost certainly have to free it and reglue it in order to position the hammer correctly in line with its strings.

If several hammer springs are broken, it is likely that the whole series should be replaced. This can be done using appropriate springy wire. Sometimes the springs are twisted round a wooden pin or cord, and sometimes they are embedded in two holes in the butt (Fig. 33). There is no magic solution to the difficulty of replacing either, but patient work with long-nosed pliers will eventually win through and a knack will be acquired. The pins or cords are usually only pressed in and can be pushed out and replaced with pieces of toothpick or similar splints. The hammer springs of modern actions catch in cord loops glued into the butts, and of course these cords must be

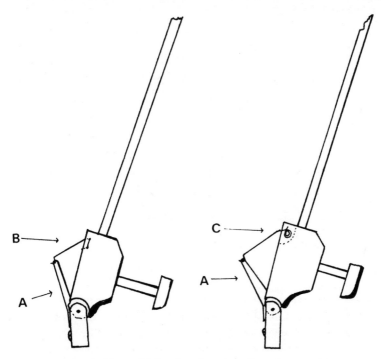

A. Loop of silk cord glued to hammer flange
B. Hammer spring enters centre of butt and comes out to form a 'stitch' on the side.
C. Hammer spring coiled round central splint or cord in butt

Fig. 33. Mounting of hammer springs

replaced if they are worn or broken. The grooves containing the old ends can be cleaned out with a piece of old hacksaw blade and then you have to insert new loops, for example of button thread or fine nylon cord, into them and apply glue. It can be difficult to make all the loops the same size. It helps to remove an intact loop with some care and to cut a supply of new loops to this length, then ensuring that they precisely fit the slots in the flange.

The other essential work on the hammers (besides the centres, where a good fit is particularly important) is on the butts and balances. The butts have felt cushions for the jacks to rest upon. These must be in good condition and come right up to the pad which forms the face of the butt notch. The

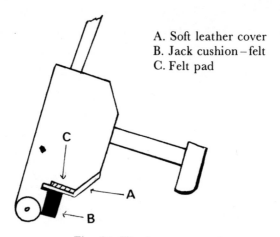

A. Soft leather cover
B. Jack cushion – felt
C. Felt pad

Fig. 34. The hammer notch

absence or partial absence of these felts, and consequent click-
ing of the jack on the wooden butt, is one of the commonest
causes of strange noises in elderly uprights. The pad itself is
covered with soft leather which is not usually worn, though it
may need restoring with sandpaper. Ensure, however, that it
or any replacement comes right down behind the cushion,
where there is usually a groove to receive its end (Fig. 34).
Where the pad has a dip through the recurrent pressure of the
jack, insert felt behind the leather to raise up the surface.
Balances nowadays are covered with soft leather, but formerly
were covered with felt. Replacing whichever you have presents
no problems. Where the tapes are breaking or broken off, they
will have to be replaced. This position varies slightly from
model to model but the replacement should be placed identi-
cally as the position affects leverage on the hammer. If the tapes
have been glued into the butts or balances along with the
balance shanks it is not worth removing the shanks. Glue the
tape as near to position as you can with an impact adhesive.
Old tape tips were of cardboard or other material which
becomes brittle and breaks up when they are disturbed. Some
later plastic tips also become hard and intractable and are made
inconveniently wide. If you cannot obtain commercial tips, soft
leather, punched through when tape and tip are glued, goes
quite well.

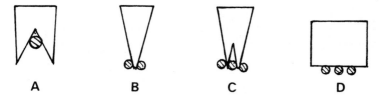

A. Clip; used for all covered monochords
B. Wedge; used for covered bichords
C. Split wedge; used for last two or three steel trichords at the break
D. Parallel; used for the steel trichords

Fig. 35. Shapes of damper felts

Dampers

On an elderly piano you are likely to find that some or all the felts need renewal. Complete replacement with makeshift felts is best avoided; confine yourself to the really bad ones even if the result is various shades of grey. It can be worth turning existing felts round so that the former middle edge, which is usually in reasonable shape, gives a cleaner and firmer top edge. If you have commercial felts, follow the pattern used before; there will be single clip felt for the monochords, simple wedge for the bichords, probably two or three split wedges for the heavier steels at the 'break', and the remainder will be soft parallel felt cut from sheet. (*See* Fig. 35 *and* Plate 10). A very sharp trimming knife is needed for cutting the angles at the end of each damper and for removing old felt (when methylated spirits may also help). It is usual to back the dampers with thin red felt. The parallel felts are apt to lose their shape unless restrained and so in many cases these felts will be found to have a single line of stitching across their middles. The ends of the stitches do not need to be fastened, so you can run down a strip of felt with a sewing machine before cutting the individual dampers from it. If you are not going to stitch, try to find a slightly firmer felt for these dampers if the originals were stitched.

Damper springs are important as not only controlling the

109

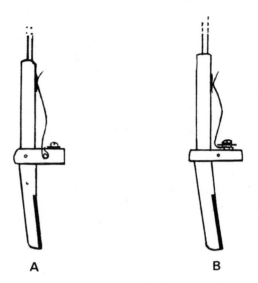

A. Normal mounting – wire coiled round splint or cord in flange
B. Improvised mounting – wire coiled round flange screw

Fig. 36. Mounting of damper springs

damping but also having considerable influence on touch. There are usually two or three gauges of spring wire in one piano and you should keep the changes in the same place even if your own wire is not identical; older damper springs were brass, whereas you may well replace them with finer gauge steel. There are several ways of mounting the springs but most often they are coiled round a cord or splint and the ends are anchored in the flange (as with hammer springs, Fig. 33). The springs, especially if brass, often crack without actually breaking, so it is well to check them carefully because a good clean damper action is most desirable. It is simplest to push out the cord or splint, coil a new spring, and then to insert the splint through the coil with it in place; it is very difficult to replace a spring without removing the splint. Try to choose a splint which will stay in place without glue or you will make things very difficult for your successors working on the piano. When it seems impossible to anchor a new spring firmly, make it so that its coil goes into the angle of the damper and flange, and the anchoring end can be turned and clamped beneath the flange screw when the damper is screwed on (Fig. 36).

While you are attending to the dampers, replace any worn or missing felt buttons beneath the tips of the damper springs. Also replace the damper tail covering (where the spoon rubs) if it is worn, with hard felt or soft leather. If there are screws into the tails behind the covers, do not alter them at this stage. Do not make the connection between the damper block (with the fixing screw to the rod) and damper head rigid; a little freedom is intended, to allow the damper to follow the string. When you have finished the dampers, take the sustaining rod off the main action rail and rub it down with steel wool. Replace it and check that it moves freely. Sometimes it has a spring, which should be cleaned up and slightly greased. More often, the damper tails alone keep it down.

Wippens, Checks and Jacks

The final major part is the wippen, together with spoon, check and jack. The foot will differ according to the capstan. If, as in modern actions, the key capstan is a brass screw, the foot will be covered with leather or felt, which should be replaced as needed. If the old type of capstan is fitted, with a dowel and felt cap, the wippen foot will be wood, black-leaded. This should be rubbed with graphite and polished with hard felt. Many older actions used a link ('abstract' or 'prolongue') between wippen and capstan and this will need similar treatment. (Some superior actions have the foot sprung to the wippen and distanced by a set-screw. Regulation is by this screw rather than the capstan.) Spoons do not deteriorate, save for a spot of rust which can easily be removed, but occasionally rough handling causes the back tip of the wippen to break off, leaving the spoon loose or in the bottom of the piano. This is an annoying fault for which there is really no satisfactory repair save for a new wippen, which is unlikely to be available. You can make a new tip for the wippen, sawing off the old one and mortising the new piece into place, or you can try for a strong joint with epoxy resin, but even then it is as well to mark the wippen for your purposes at the front so that you treat it with special caution when regulating the damper. The jack must be

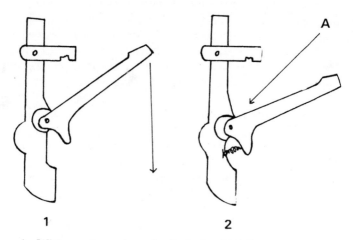

A

1. Without the spring, the jack should fall under its own weight
2. The spring should just lift the jack until it stops against the wippen

Fig. 37. Testing jack centre and spring

free on its centre. Take out the spring and test that the jack will fall from a horizontal position by its own weight; if not, it is too tight. Jack springs occasionally fall out when an action is handled with the tapes disconnected. They also become compressed. The spring should just raise the jack as far as it can go with the wippen held vertical (Fig. 37). It is not difficult to coil a new spring from fine wire and it can be given a spot of glue where it seats in the wippen, but not where it meets the jack. The checks and check wires screw in. An extra couple of turns to tighten them will do no harm but there is a danger of splitting the wood. Epoxy resin can be used if the wood is damaged. The check felts will need cleaning and picking up. As a rule they wear only when the balance is worn also. The felt is easily replaced. In all this work, which is very dirty, I find the best cleaning tools are a substantial paint brush and a small wire suede brush for hard felt and rusted wires.

112

ASSEMBLY AND REGULATION

Do not put the action back together completely and expect all to be well. It probably will not be. It is best to start by screwing on only the dampers. Place the action in the piano and adjust the dampers to align with the strings. If a damper does not press on its string, check that, if there is a screw in the damper tail to press on the sustaining rod, it is not too far advanced and preventing the damper from reaching the string. If there are no screws, the damper wires must be bent until the dampers line up and press on their strings – run your finger over the strings in order to identify those sounding free of their dampers. When all is well, connect up the sustaining pedal rod and check that when the pedal is depressed all the dampers rise in a straight line parallel with the strings and action. Those that move ahead of the others can have their wires bent, but ensuring that they still press on the strings without the pedal. If the screws are present, they are of course adjusted so that the dampers rise evenly with the pedal. Once you have set up the dampers in this way any further adjustments to them should be made only by means of the damper spoons because it will only be regulation to the keys that is required.

Your principal concern with the hammers – which of course you may meanwhile have recovered (*see* Chapter 7) – is their alignment with the strings. Screw on the hammer rail and the hammers whilst the action is still in the piano. There is often slight play between flange and action rail so that, by loosening their screws, you may be able to correct crooked hammers. Failing this, place sellotape or plastic insulating tape under one side of the flange in order to tip the hammer to the opposite side. Now is of course the time to fit on any hammer heads where you have replaced the shanks.

The wippens you can replace only with the action out of the piano, It can be a fiddly job to clear the spoons with your screwdriver when the dampers are in place, but it is much better to have the dampers basically regulated without the wippens and hammers to complicate matters. (Special screwdrivers are in fact made for this job, or you can modify the shoulders of an ordinary screwdriver with a narrow shaft.) For replacing the wippens, you will need the rack or the blocks again to protect the rest of the action on the bench. Once you have the wippens on, turn the action round and start connecting the tapes. Whilst you do so, take care to raise the jacks so that they fall on to their felt. You will have found some cushions unevenly worn, probably, because the jacks were not central. Try to make these central, if necessary by tilting the flanges as you did the hammer flanges, but make sure that the wippens are evenly spaced, or the capstans will not align with the wippens. Adjust the bridle wires and tapes by bending. The tapes which you replaced or re-tipped may well not be of quite correct length. The jacks should be quite free, but the tapes should not permit the jacks to fall below their cushions. Take a look at the position of the jack before pressing up a wippen which seems to hang low; probably the jack has so fallen and in that case you will damage the cushion if you force the wippen up without at the same time lifting the jack tip. You have to bend the bridle wires until the tapes allow the jacks just a little – 2 mm or so – movement when the action is out. The check wires can be bent so that the hammer balances fall squarely on to them, but do not at this stage bend the wires in or out and, when bending them, be careful to hold the wippens firmly to avoid breakages.

Now replace the action in the piano and check the strike distance to 50 mm, screwing the standard bearing-bolts in or out if necessary; change is especially likely to be needed if you have recovered the hammers. Adjust the key capstans or dowels up or down until there is minute freedom of the jack tip in the butt notch before it takes on the weight of the hammer, and until all the hammer shanks just rest on the hammer rail.

You have now to adjust the invisible damper spoons so that each note's damper rises at the same stage of key depression, and so that this moment is the best time from the point of view of touch. As has been mentioned, there is some latitude here, but generally dampers should move when the hammers are half-way to striking or the key is not quite half down. You can bend the spoons with the cranked slotted tool (Plate 1b) with the action in place, but hold the wippens firmly when you do so. This method requires practice but is really the easier one. Alternatively, set the bottom damper as required and then mark in one way all those dampers which move earlier, and in another way all those which move later; self-adhesive coloured blobs applied to the wippens are a clear and easy way of doing this. Then you take out the action and bend the spoons appropriately, and repeat the process possibly several times, testing and re-marking on each occasion, till all is well.

Regulate the set-off or escapement with the slotted tool; striking the keys, turn the screws downwards to make escapement occur earlier or upwards to delay escapement. As has been said, set-off should be as close to the string as possible, but 2 mm will be about as near as you can come without the hammers 'blocking' on the strings, and there must be no chance of this. The checks are adjusted by bending the wires in or out (again, holding the wippens firmly) until the hammers check, as you strike the keys and hold them down, some 20 mm from the strings. Use a slotted tool for bending and proceed two or three keys at a time so that the hammers all check at the same distance from the strings.

The sustaining pedal should present no problem if your dampers have been correctly set up. Allow about 8 mm free movement of the pedal when adjusting its screw. The soft pedal should be adjusted to give an acceptable 'half blow'. When you press down the soft pedal there should not normally be any movement of the wippens. If there is movement of isolated wippens, their tapes are too short. If there is general movement, you may be reducing the strike to less than a half blow. If there is no room for adjustment at the pedal you can insert or reduce washers at the pedal rod. In some old pianos where the actions were heavy, the keys would drop forward when the weight of the hammers was taken by the soft pedal and then of course movement of the wippens cannot be avoided. When you apply the soft pedal, you increase the gap between jack tip and hammer butt; this 'lost motion' (Fig. 38) is undesirable but the devices invented to eliminate it are too expensive ever to have been produced on a large scale.

A final question which you may have to consider has been left to last because, though important, in a great many cases no adjustment is required. This is the height of the action against strings and keys, which is considered at the end of

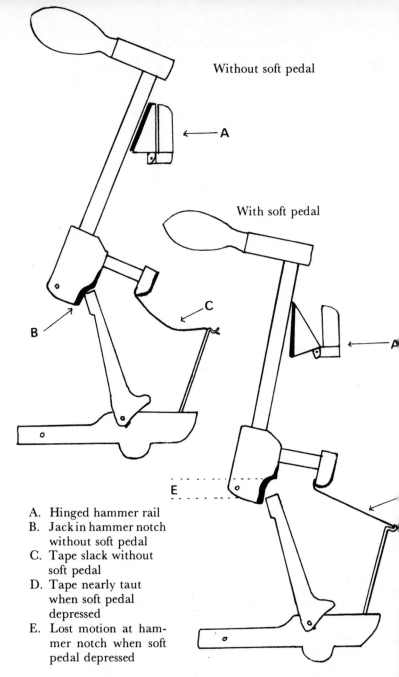

Without soft pedal

With soft pedal

A. Hinged hammer rail
B. Jack in hammer notch without soft pedal
C. Tape slack without soft pedal
D. Tape nearly taut when soft pedal depressed
E. Lost motion at hammer notch when soft pedal depressed

Fig. 38. Lost motion with the half-blow pedal

Chapter 6. If there *is* reason to doubt the original setting, or it has been tampered with, however, attention should be given to it, at least in the first instance, before regulating the key capstans. Otherwise they will all have to be altered.

Chapter Five

THE GRAND ACTION

If you are concerned with a grand action it would nevertheless be as well to read the previous chapter on upright actions, since important parts of it apply equally to grand actions and will not be repeated here. This applies particularly to what is said on centres.

Structure

The grand action is fixed to the extended key-frame by screws through the standards. Keyboard and action are therefore removed from the piano in one unit and then the action is separated for overhauling. The action is almost entirely inaccessible in the piano and therefore regulation has for the most part to be made outside the instrument, using a dummy structure to represent the line of the striking points on the strings and their height above the hammers.

As a rule, access is by lifting out the fall, unscrewing the key-blocks from underneath the key-bed, and removing the key-slip. Occasionally the key-slip, screwed below, has to be removed before the fall and key-blocks. The action is even more heavy, awkward and fragile than that of the upright, though it has the blessing that it can lie flat on the bench. The key-frame has to be held (if by one person) with hands at either end and with arms outstretched. The whole is most easily removed whilst you sit on a stool or bench with a good surface behind or beside you so that you have only to turn to place the action on it. Alternatively, and more safely, two people can carry the assembly. Be very careful not to press any of the keys whilst removing the action; if you depress a key you will raise its hammer, which can catch and be broken on the wrestplank above. Equally, when the action is out, never strike a key hard without limiting the upward movement of the hammer (for example, with a hand in its path) or you may break its shank.

The action will be found constructed on similar principles to those of the upright action (Fig. 39). It is built on two rails,

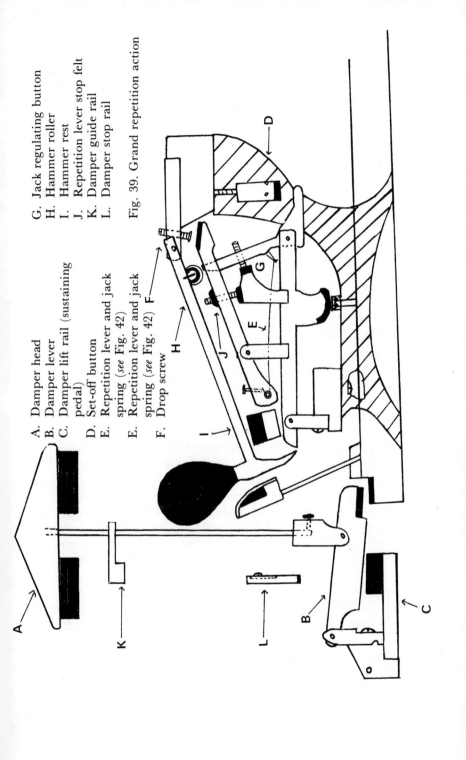

A. Damper head
B. Damper lever
C. Damper lift rail (sustaining pedal)
D. Set-off button
E. Repetition lever and jack spring (*see* Fig. 42)
E. Repetition lever and jack spring (*see* Fig. 42)
F. Drop screw

G. Jack regulating button
H. Hammer roller
I. Hammer rest
J. Repetition lever stop felt
K. Damper guide rail
L. Damper stop rail

Fig. 39. Grand repetition action

holding the wippens and the hammers and secured to four
or five iron standards. The hammer rest may be a rail also, or
there may be individual rests secured to each wippen – the rest
has a different function from the hammer rail of an upright
action. Further, the checks are fixed to the key backs, not to
the wippens, and the dampers are not attached to the action
and have to be removed separately (*see below*, 'Repairs'). The
set-off buttons or dollies are most often screwed blind into
the top rail which supports the hammers and are turned by
a prong or wire inserted into the dowel holes (as with an old
upright's dowel capstans). For clarity's sake we shall call this
large top rail the 'hammer flange rail', since 'hammer rail'
is ambiguous in relation to that part of the upright action
which supports the hammer heads. There are no damper
slap, jack slap or let-off rails, no damper springs and no hammer
springs.

(*Direct Lever and Spring and Loop Actions*)

This chapter will be mainly concerned with the 'roller' or
'repetition' action which is now universal in grands. However,
until quite recently, there was a cheaper and simpler action,
which can be traced back to Broadwood's 'English action' (so-
called on the Continent, to which it was exported) in the 19th
Century. Versions of this were probably as common as versions
of repetition action in the 19th and early 20th Centuries. In
its classic form this alternative may be called the 'single escapement' action or 'direct lever action' and is illustrated in Fig.
40. It is more like the upright action in that the jack (mounted
on the key – it is because there is no wippen that the term 'direct
lever' is used) works in a hammer butt notch. The action has
wooden standards – as do upright actions of similar vintage –
but the checks are on the keys and the mounting of the hammers
and action of the dampers are as in the roller action. There
are no tapes – since there are no wippens and gravity does not
need tapes to help it to return the hammers.

This action is overhauled and regulated by a combination
of the principles and methods applying to roller and upright
actions, and if you are familiar with these it will not cause you
any particular difficulty. The same applies to its later form in
which there are wippens and a jack and hammer spring ('spring

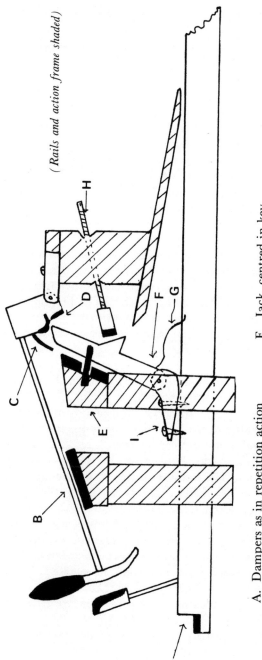

(Rails and action frame shaded)

A. Dampers as in repetition action (Fig. 39)
B. Hammer rest
C. Hammer butt, with felt slip limiting jack
D. Hammer notch
E. Jack slap rail, with felted dowels limiting jack's sideways movement

F. Jack, centred in key
G. Jack spring
H. Set-off screw button
I. Rocker and adjusting screw into key

Fig. 40. Direct lever grand action (*see* Plate 16)

and loop action') – this closely resembles the corresponding type of upright action.

As we shall see, in a roller action the hammers do not remain on their rests when the action is still. With these variants, however, which resemble upright actions, the hammers do so rest, and the capstans must be regulated, as with an upright, so that the tips of the jacks are properly in the hammer butt notch when the key is at rest and the hammer shanks are lying on their rail. The jacks in a direct lever action are centred on curved rockers fitted to the keys. There are no capstans – turning the rocker screws raises or lowers the jacks in the hammer butts. The spring and loop action has capstans like those of an upright and is adjusted similarly in this respect.

Working

Plates 11–14 depict the sequence of events in an actual (roller) action. Points to note particularly are various positions of the repetition lever (visible by observing its distance from the stop button above it) and the action of the jack. The damper cannot, of course, be shown, since it is within the piano, but this is a much simpler matter than in the underdamped upright piano and will be clear from Fig. 39.

The roller action is similar to the upright action until the hammer has struck the string and begins to return. When the action is at rest, the weight of the hammer rests not on the hammer rest but on the key, via the repetition lever and wippen (Plate 11). The pressing of the key raises the wippen and jack (which passes through a slot in the repetition lever and engages just to the front of the padded roller on the hammer shank) so raising the hammer. The hammer is driven by the jack, not by the repetition lever (save for a minute instant at the start). When the key is depressed some 3 mm (as with the upright there is some scope for variation) its back raises the damper lever and so also the damper (Fig. 39). There is no damper spring, but there is a lead weight in the lever to accelerate the damper's return by gravity when the key is released. When the hammer is very close to the string, the set-off button presses on the jack heel and forces the jack tip to separate from the hammer roller.

Operate the key very gently and hold it down. You will see

that the hammer roller next falls back on to the repetition lever and is held up there by its spring, at a height determined by the setting of the 'drop' screw. If you then release the key, the jack slides in beneath the roller again (Plate 12). If you depress the key hard enough for the hammer to strike the string – or your hand if the action is out – and you hold the key down, the hammer should rebound with sufficient force to depress the repetition lever and fall until its roughened tail catches on the check at the back of the key (Plate 13). When you now partly release the key, the sprung repetition lever will raise the hammer so that the jack can relocate on the hammer roller and you can sound the note again without having fully released the key (Plate 14). This is the purpose of the repetition lever and the main superiority of the roller action over upright and direct lever or non-repetition grand actions. If, on the other hand, you had quickly released the key, the hammer would have passed the check and bounced on the hammer rest, rising very slightly to its normal position above the rest as the key was released. The damper, meanwhile, would have reacted according to the position of the key.

REPAIRS

Making a Regulating Bar

Before you can regulate the action you must make a structure to represent the correct distance (the usual 50 mm) of the hammers from the strings and to simplify aligning the hammers, for both processes are virtually impossible with the action in the piano. You require a stout straight-edge as wide as the keyframe, and two uprights to stand on the edges of the frame. It is essential that the edges do not droop, so use substantial wood (or metal if you can work with it). If you do not propose to re-cover or alter the hammers, the straight-edge can be fixed to the tops of the upright pieces in such a way that it is at 90° to them and is 50 mm above the top treble hammer. However, you may wish to re-cover or reshape the heads, and you have to allow for the higher overstrung hammers in any case, so it is best to make the structure adjustable. Make slots in the uprights and use bolts and wing-nuts to secure the straight-edge, and put slots in the bar as well to accommodate

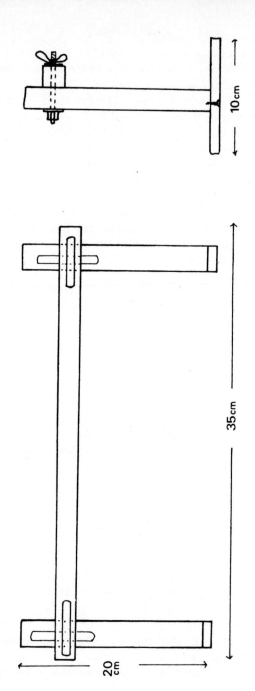

35 cm

20 cm

Fig. 41. Regulating bar for grands

slightly different widths of action standard for future use (Fig. 41).

When you place the bar over the hammers, set it and screw it up firmly, then mark on the key-frame the exact place where the uprights are to rest. This is to enable you to replace all the hammers in line with their strings (assuming that they were in line previously) after dismantling. Having thus established the position of the bar, depress each key gently in turn, being careful not to move the bar, and mark on the bar the precise position of both sides of the raised hammer head. For clarity's sake, shade between these marks to show the width of the hammers. Use chalk if the bar is to be employed again.

Hammers

Remove the bar, which is not now needed until reassembly, and then unscrew the standards and separate the action from the key-frame, having first established that you have not one of the few actions in which the key capstans are linked to the wippens (in which case they must first be freed). Then remove the hammers one by one.

Check each hammer for excessive side-travel in the centre and then examine the rollers. These are wooden splints set into the shanks, wrapped round with a cushion and protected by soft leather. They are not easy to replace and I suggest leaving them alone unless there is severe wear or actual breakage. If you do have to repair any, use a slightly longer slip of leather and press it into the corners on the shanks with a knife, not trimming it off until the glue has set. There should be no glue on the leather, inside or out, save at these corners. Reconditioning of the hammer heads is described in Chapter 7. The wooden hammer tails have to be rough where they engage with the checks. For this a coarse rasp or a few superficial saw-cuts will suffice. Broken shanks must be replaced or repaired as in Chapter 4. Leave fitting the heads until the action is assembled and they can be glued on in line. As there will be no markings on the bar, make the shanks a push-fit so that you can try them under their actual strings before finally glueing the heads on.

Wippens and Carriages

Remove the wippens, which carry the jacks and repetition lever assemblies (sometimes known as the 'carriages'), and lay them out in order. As with the upright action, it is prudent to number them from bottom to top, if they have not already been numbered, and to keep them with their screws. Then treat the wippens one by one, examining and if necessary replacing the various felt pads with felt of exactly the same thickness and density as far as possible, and paying particular attention to every centre. You may need to do no more than clean up the wippens. On the other hand, you may have to replace the lever stop felts, which will mean punching out the lever's centre to free it, or to replace a cracked or broken repetition spring. The design and strength of these springs varies. Most often there is one spring bent round a pin in the tail of the lever and tightened by means of a grub-screw. This wire passes through the support for the lever stop felts and screw, and on towards the jack, where it catches on a cord loop. Alternatively, a 'V'-shaped spring, with a coil in the middle, connects jack and lever directly (since the pressure is required in opposite directions), springing them against each other. Occasionally, separate springs are used for the jack and the lever, with separate loops. Whatever the system, it is very important to replace with wire of as nearly as possible identical character, or one unit of the action will always stand out against the others in performance. The action will be fitted with several grades of spring, since they are related to the varying weights of the hammers from treble to bass. The loops can be repaired as those for hammer springs in the previous chapter. Fig. 42 shows the two main systems of springing.

When you have repaired and reassembled a wippen and carriage, set it up so that it will need as little regulation later as possible; have the lever adjusted so that it is just a paper's thickness higher than the jack tip, and set the jack stop as it was, or so that the tip aligns with a maker's mark on the lever which shows where the tip engages with the hammer roller. If all is well, the back edge of the tip will then be just in front of the roller's splint when the hammer is replaced.

Action Rails

Clean up the rails and attend to the regulating buttons as necessary. As a rule, there is little to be done to the rails save for re-covering a hammer rest with soft cushion felt if it is badly

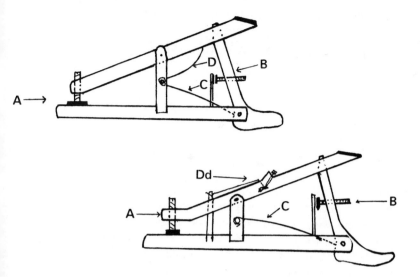

A. Repetition lever stop felt
B. Jack regulating button
C. Jack spring
D. Repetition lever spring
Dd.Repetition lever spring working on silk cord attached to wippen and passing through lever

Fig. 42. Alternative forms of repetition lever and jack springs.

worm or indented. Either mark the height-setting of the hammer rest, or leave the lower screw untouched if you are using very similar felt. Otherwise, compensate for the difference, since the rest must be set so as to receive the hammer on rebound but not to support it when still.

Setting Up Jacks and Hammers

Refit the wippens – a point to watch for is that no adjacent repetition levers rub at the tops; rubbing produces a noise hard to trace and of course impairs performance. Refit the hammers, replace the action on the key-frame, and set up your regulating bar so that you can exactly align the hammers with the marks on the bar. You have now to check that the jacks align

127

perfectly with the hammer rollers – this is most easily done by pressing down the repetition levers slightly to reveal the jacks. If the jacks do not align, loosen the affected wippens and move them on their flange screws, inserting self-adhesive tape (as when aligning uprights' hammers) if necessary to one side. Make sure the wippens are well screwed home. If they come loose, they produce elusive clicks, and of course they are completely inaccessible within the piano.

Dampers

Remove the dampers themselves by undoing the grub-screws in the cylindrical damper-blocks (within the piano, behind the action). Hold the wires as you undo the screws, or you risk bending them. Lay out all the dampers in order, polish their wires with metal polish, and service the felts as noted for uprights in Chapter 4. Remove the damper lever rail with all its assemblies and check the centres of the damper levers. If you replace the lever (or key) felts it must be with the same thickness of felt or damper response will be erratic. Remove the lift rail (for the sustaining pedal) and clean or re-cover it. You can then reinstate all except the dampers with their wires.

A crucial part in the grand damper apparatus is the guide rail, a thin slip of wood pierced with felt bushings for the damper wire, and mounted on the front edge of the sound-board. If notes are prolonged and dampers come down too slowly as keys are released, the trouble is likely to be here. The same is true if a damper wobbles and vibrates on its strings. Closely observe the fit of each damper wire as you pass it through the guide prior to reassembly, and then check the damper's seating by plucking the strings with the damper on them. If the wire is at all tight, the bushing will have to be very slightly loosened. Try first warming the wire and sliding it to and fro in the hole. If this fails, choose a piece of wire of the same size, roughen it with emery or on a file, and repeat the sliding, warming also if necessary. Be most wary of overdoing the job. If, as is common with old grands (especially with the monochords), the bushings are worn through or partly missing, they will have to be replaced. It is possible to do this with the strings and frame in place but it is naturally simpler if the strings happen to be removed. It may also be possible to remove the

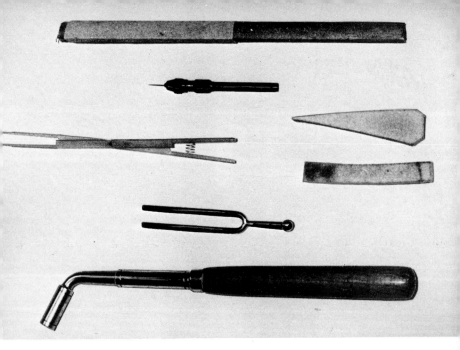

1. (*above*) Tools for Tuning and Toning (in descending order) Sand file; Toning needle in pin vice; Papp mutes (felt mutes to right); Tuning fork; Tuning lever (goose-necked).
(*below*) Miscellaneous Tools
Top Upright damper regulating tool
Centre row, l. to r. Grand damper regulating tool; Slotted regulating tool (*above*); String lifting and spacing lever (*below*); Cantilever string cutters.
Bottom Torque wrench.

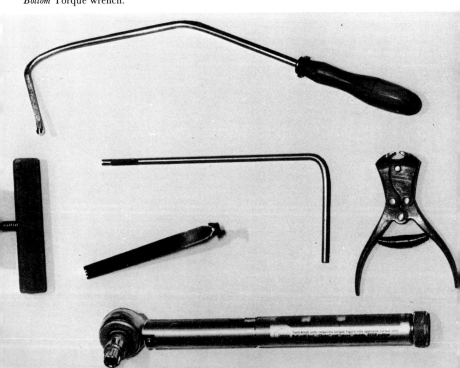

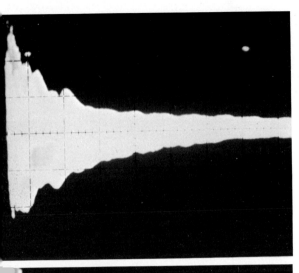

2. Oscillographs (*see* Chapter 2)
a. Middle C, Onset and Decay with note held down (Each vertical division on the scale represents 0.2 secs)

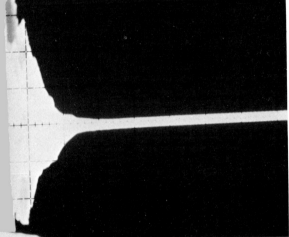

b. Middle C, Staccato (Time-scale as 2a)

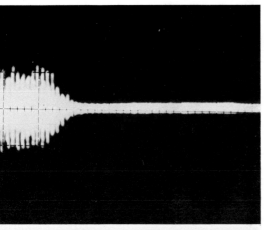

3. Oscillographs (cont.)
a. Bottom C, Staccato
(Each vertical division on the scale represents 0.2 secs)

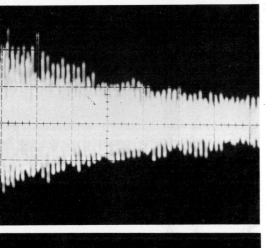

b. Bottom C, Onset and Decay – with note held down (Time-scale as 3*a*)

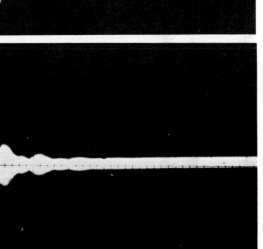

c. Top C, Onset and Decay – with note held down (Each vertical division on the scale represents 5 m/secs)

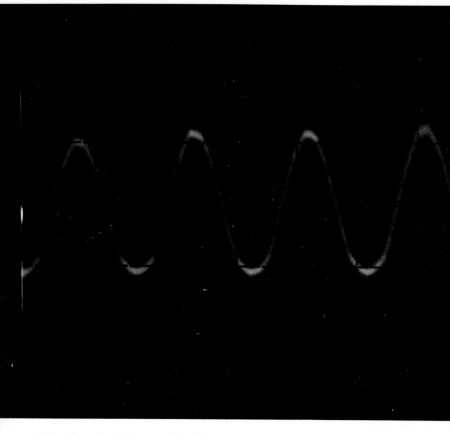

4. Electronically Generated Sine Wave

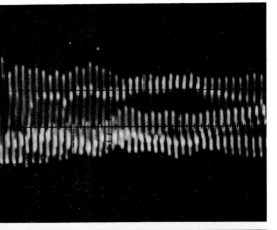

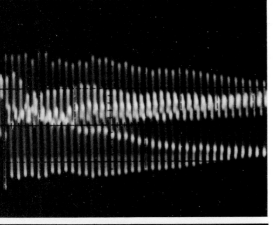

5. The effect of different Hammer Felts

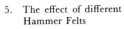

a. Soft felt

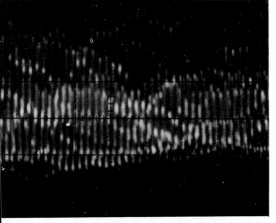

b. good toned felt

c. very hard felt

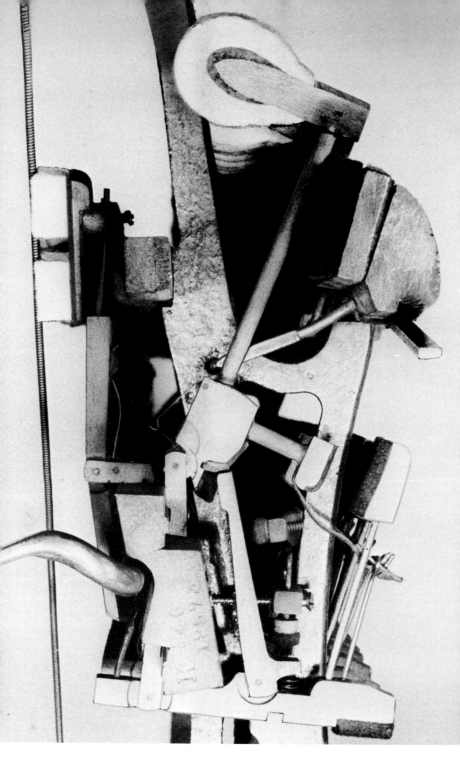

6. The Upright Action at rest (*see* Fig. 28)

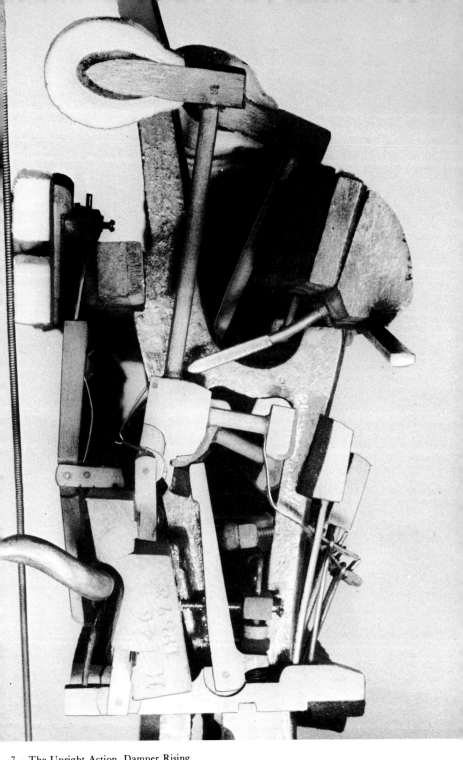

7. The Upright Action, Damper Rising

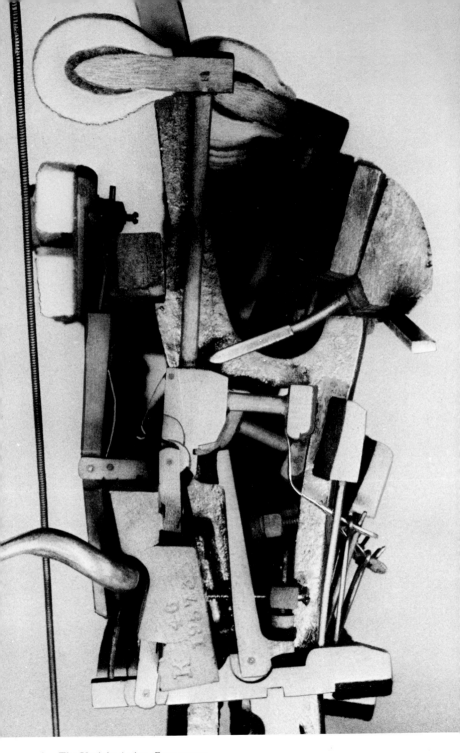

8. The Upright Action, Escapement

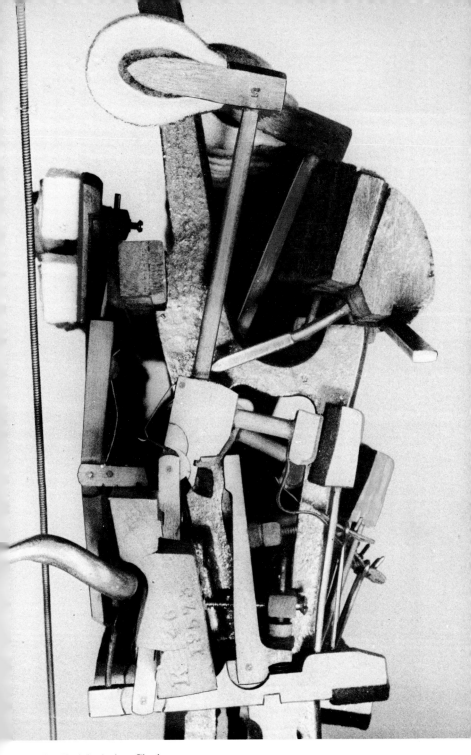

9. The Upright Action, Check

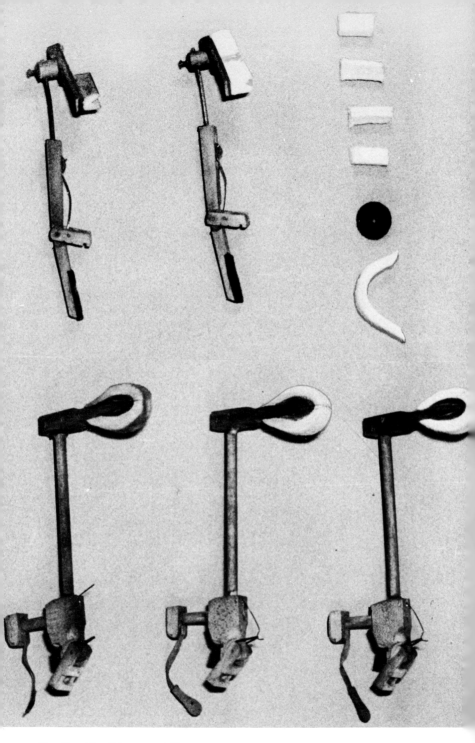

10. Repairing Dampers and Hammers
    Top, l. to r. Damper before repair, After repair, Miscellaneous felts (four shaped damper felt, one key felt button, one hammer felt ready for glueing)
    Bottom, l. to r. Hammer ready for repair, Hammer reshaped, Hammer hand-covered

11.   The Grand Action at rest (*see* Fig. 39)

12. The Grand Action, Escapement and Drop

13.   The Grand Action, Check

14. The Grand Action, ready for repetition

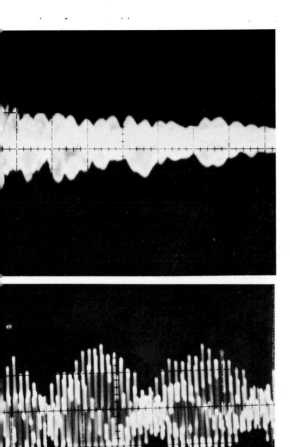

15*a*. Beats in poorly tuned unison (Each vertical division on the scale represents 0.1 secs)

15b. Detail of beats at higher speed

16. Direct Lever Grand Action (Broadwood) (*See* Fig. 40)

guide rail with the strings in place, unscrewing from above and poking it through to fall on the key-bed. If you do so, put new felt between its mounting blocks and the sounding board. The new bushings are put in with a corner of cloth, as when doing the flanges, and when they are in place you will have to test all over again. Where the wood round the hole is worn, you can use a thicker bushing, but it is better to plug the hole solid and then to drill and bush it afresh. It is essential that the dampers fall rapidly but smoothly and be unable to move on their strings. It must be said, however, that it is sometimes impossible to eliminate all variation in the performance of grand dampers. They seem particularly subject to changes in humidity.

Setting Up the Dampers

If the keyboard is in order (*see* the next Chapter), it is now possible to fit and regulate the dampers using the home-made tool described in Chapter 1. This is done before replacing the action in the piano. Place the tool on the table or bench at the back of the key-frame and adjust the movable slip of wood until it just rests on the keys' damper felts when the keys are down at the back. This slip was deliberately chosen for its thickness of 3 mm. You now move the gadget to the key-bed and insert the slip between two or three damper levers. This will hold them the required distance above the keys, when the latter are replaced. Let the dampers lie on the strings with the wires loose, and then tighten the screws in their blocks (Fig. 43). Depress the sustaining pedal so that the damper lift rail raises all the dampers, and then fit the stop rail above the levers allowing about 2 mm above this highest position for the dampers.

Regulation

With the action restored to the key-frame and the hammer heads aligned with their marks on the regulating bar, check at intervals that the distance of the heads (i.e. the strike distance) is 50 mm from the bar and that they are in a horizontal line until you reach the overstrung hammers, when approximately 15 mm has to be added (or the bar raised that amount) since these hammers also travel 50 mm. (Note that the strike distance in Steinway grands is 47 mm). Adjust this strike

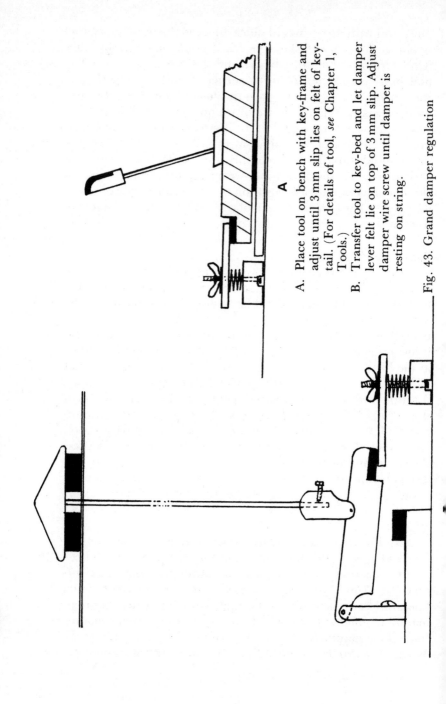

A. Place tool on bench with key-frame and adjust until 3 mm slip lies on felt of key-tail. (For details of tool, *see* Chapter 1, Tools.)

B. Transfer tool to key-bed and let damper lever felt lie on top of 3 mm slip. Adjust damper wire screw until damper is resting on string.

Fig. 43. Grand damper regulation

distance by screwing the capstans up or down as needed. Having done this, check that the hammer rest (if not attached to the wippens) is clear of the shanks by some 3 mm, and alter the mounting nuts as necessary. Next, although you make a preliminary check when servicing the wippens, press down each repetition lever to establish that the jack tips are just in front of the splints of the hammer rollers. If they are not, adjust them by the jack regulating buttons.

You can now adjust the escapement, using the bar as your string. As a rule, set-off can be set more finely on a grand than on an upright and it should be possible to secure reliable escapement when the hammer head is 2 mm or even less from the string, without there being any danger of blocking or bouncing on the string. Immediately following escapement, the hammer drops on to the repetition lever – at speed, of course, it takes the lever down with itself. Test the action by a very gentle key movement so that the hammer does not actually depress the lever but just drops on to it. It should drop little more than 2 mm. Unless you have replaced the levers' felt tips or have altered the drop screws, it probably will do so, since this is not a setting which normally needs to be altered. Adjustment is of course by the drop screw. If the 'drop' is exessive, the jack may fail to relocate under the hammer roller, so that repetition will be poor; if it is too small the hammer will block on the string.

Passing on to the return of the hammers, cause each hammer in turn to strike the bar and then to rebound into check. If you hold the key down, the hammer should stay caught on the check. If it does not, you have either to roughen the check further or to bend it in, though not so far that the hammer touches it when rising. Bend the check wires so that all the hammers are caught at the same distance, about 20 mm, from the strings. Once this is satisfactory, repeat the process, but this time half-releasing each key. If the hammer gently rises up to full repetition lever height, well and good. If it jumps up and strikes the bar, the repetition spring is exerting too great a force and must be adjusted either by bending or by its adjusting screw if present. Of course, if the hammer barely rises or is very sluggish, the reverse adjustment is needed. Also if it is very difficult to make the hammer stay in check, consider the possibility that the repetition lever is too strong.

Replacing the Action

All should now be well for you to replace the action in the piano in confidence that the normally inaccessible jobs have been done. Adjust the pedals, with their respective rods and if necessary by changing the felt or leather pads, so that they travel about 8 mm before the dampers start to rise or the action shifts. Check that the stop on the treble key-block is set correctly so that, when the soft pedal is used, one string of each group (save for monochords) is missed by the hammers. Do not alter the stops behind the action which position it beneath the strings. They govern the strike line. It is most unlikely that the strike line was incorrectly set in the first place or has been altered since, and there is not the tendency for it to alter as with the dropping of the action which can occur in an upright.

Chapter Six

THE KEYBOARD

It is rather easy to lay aside a keyboard of which the covers are not chipped and to assume that all is well. Obviously the keyboard is the most viewed part of the piano and the one in which gross disrepair is most immediately visible. But it is also a most sensitive part of the instrument where touch is concerned, it is liable to be attacked by moth and to harbour all sorts of unsavoury things invisibly, and it is extremely subject to wear although outwardly robust. A piano in which the sounding parts and action are in tip-top condition but the keys are sloppy, unpredictable or not in conformity with standard measurements is, for all practical purposes, in a bad way. Time spent on a keyboard is time well spent.

Structure

The term 'keyboard' refers particularly to the keys themselves; they are in fact cut from one solid board and you will find certain slots cut in some keys which are unnecessary but are needed in other keys, and so have been cut 'across the board'. The keyboard is literally balanced on the key-frame, a strongly constructed wooden rectangle with a back rail, a front rail and a raised centre or balance rail on which the keys pivot (Fig. 44).

We have seen that the key-frame and action of a grand are removed by sliding out from the front of the instrument. They are not fixed to the key-bed, but closely placed between back stops and key-slip so that the whole can slide along for soft pedal action. The key-frame of an upright is screwed into the key-bed with screws through the frame's rails and cross members, which vary in number. Where these screws are, you cannot discover until you remove the keys which conceal most of them. As a rule the exact height of the key-frame above the key-bed is set by shims of wood or cardboard. There is something to be said for leaving these in place for the time being since the

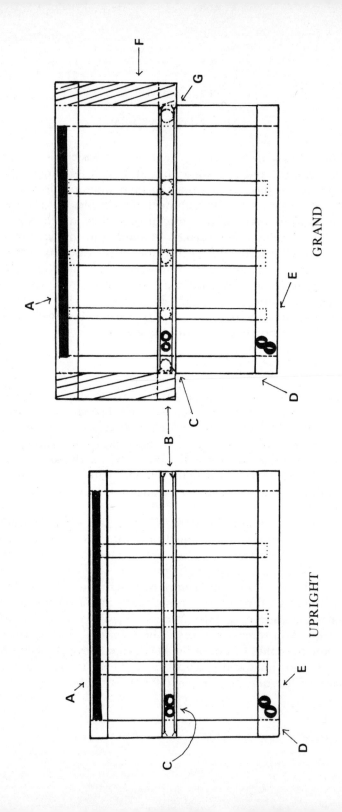

GRAND

UPRIGHT

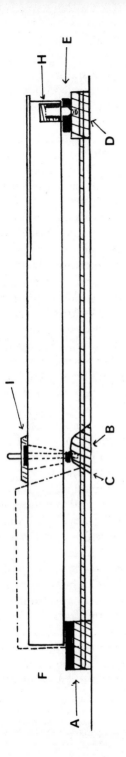

A. Back rail and felt
B. Balance rail
C. Centre/Balance pins with felts governing height of keys
D. Front rail
E. Oval/bat pins with felt buttons governing depth of touch
F. Raised edges on the grand key-frame, to support action standards
G. Polished glides on underside of grand key-frame
H. Front bushing round oval pin
I. Key-chase and balance rail bushing round balance pin

Fig. 44. Key-frames

height is critical and you may not have to do anything to the key-frame which will demand altering the shims.

The balance rail has screwed into it round polished pins which go through the centre holes of the keys. Around each pin, between key and rounded rail, is a felt washer. The front rail is similarly studded, but the pins are oval and have much thicker washers on them to absorb the impact of the keys when depressed. This shape of the pins is to limit the friction fore and aft, although a by-product is that they can be turned a little to tighten their fit in the front key holes if needed. The back rail is covered with a thick absorbent baize. Removed from the action, the keys may 'balance forward' or 'balance backwards'. If the keys tip forwards they do so to take account of the considerable weight of the action, so that the touch appears normal. Grand keys balance forwards, and so do keys of older pianos having 'abstracts' or 'prolongues' between the key capstans and the wippens. Nowadays with uprights, backwards balancing is usual and as a rule lead has to be inserted at the back to add to the weight given by the action, for the standard proportions of the keys in fact dispose them to balance forwards unweighted. Keys balanced forwards may also have weights in them, at the front, to counteract the action's weight. These weights should not be removed or supplemented save as a last resort; there is something very wrong if so basic a part of the manufacturer's design needs to be modified. The standard key proportions referred to are (for naturals) three parts in front of the balance pin and two parts behind it for uprights, and two parts in front of the balance and one part between balance and capstan for grands. There are also of course standard measurements for playing surfaces and the height of the key fronts, but as we shall not be making a new key there is no need to itemize them.

The white keys are known as 'whites' or 'naturals' and the black keys are always referred to as 'sharps'. The sharps should be about 12 mm higher than the naturals (at the front). The height of the balance rail in relation to the back rail is such that the keys slope up towards the front and are horizontal when half-depressed. Whilst the height for the rails is largely determined by the action and the striking-point of the hammers, it is obviously undesirable for the key bottoms to be visible along

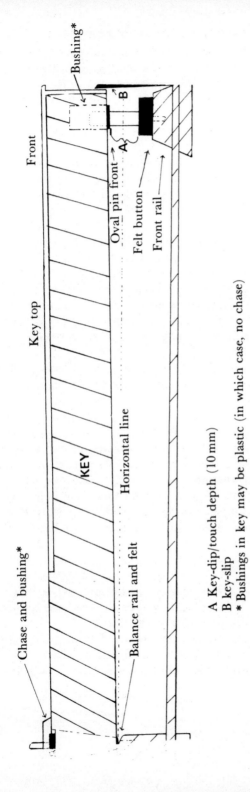

Chase and bushing*

Bushing*

Front

Key top

KEY

Oval pin front

B

A

Felt button

Front rail

Horizontal line

Balance rail and felt

A Key-dip/touch depth (10 mm)
B key-slip
* Bushings in key may be plastic (in which case, no chase)

Fig. 45 Key and key-dip (Scale drawing)

the line of the key-slip, and in practice the key-slip usually covers the key fronts by 2–3 mm (Fig. 45).

The keys are merely dropped on to their balance pins although, as the recoil of grand hammers makes the keys jump up, grands have a thin strip of felted rail set above the keys, just behind the fall, to limit their upward movement. Each key has two important bushing points, one at the centre hole and one at the front – these bushes have until very recently been felt but are now sometimes made of plastic. Their purpose is of course to limit movement and noise. The centre bush is covered by a wooden 'chase' to hold it in place although this is not used with plastic bushes. Nearly all keys have a 'capstan' (there are various names) of some type. The modern tendency is to use a brass screw with a hexagonal head or with 'capstan' holes in the head, and this is usual with grands. Older, bigger uprights used either a dowel capstan raised on a screwed rod, or a felt pad on the key engaging with a capstan screw at the bottom of the 'prolongue' (Fig. 46). A rocker or rider is used where the wippen is linked to the key or where there is no wippen.

Modern naturals are covered in various types of plastic. The highest quality coverings are ivory. On older pianos these are usual and can be distinguished by being in three parts for each key (owing to difficulties in cutting them in one piece) and for having a rather irregular fine grain. Metal polish is the best radical cleaner for keys which are stained rather than merely grubby, but it leaves them dull and you need a power buff to restore them, though some good can be done with hard felt. Tripoli is a still more drastic cleaner. Use it lubricated with oil. The tops of sharps may be wood or plastic. If wood they can be restored with thin black lacquer applied thinly so that it does not run.

Repairs

Number all the keys, from the bottom, as you remove them. Often you will find that they have already been stamped. Then put them aside and turn to the frame.

On all but a modern piano every felt has to be removed for cleaning, even if new felts are not fitted throughout. A keyboard and frame harbour an enormous amount of dust. As a rule the

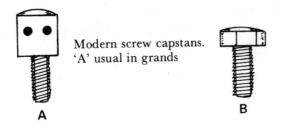

Modern screw capstans. 'A' usual in grands

A

B

Old dowel capstan for larger uprights

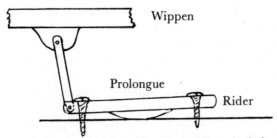

Wippen

Prologue

Rider

Linkage found in 'tied actions' where wippen is tied to key by prologue. The rider pivots on domed underside for adjustment.

Fig. 46. Key capstans.

back rail felt will need to be replaced because it has been compressed by the keys. Its original thickness, observable between the keys, has to be restored. On the other two rails there are felt punchings and also paper ones. The paper ones have been used in setting the keys level and adjusting the depth of touch. Whilst there may be more than one punching on many balance rail pins, try to establish from a pin with one punching what the basic requirement is as to thickness, and start cutting out a large number of similar punchings if you have not obtained them from the supplier. The felt buttons on the front rail pins are of a standard thickness, and you may have to cut a great many circles in order to build up to this for every note if you cannot get proper felt washers. Or you may decide that not every punching needs to be replaced. Whatever the verdict, have them all off – one by one if you want to preserve the original setting – and inspect the pins. These must be entirely free of rust and it is best to polish them with metal polish.

Observe the condition of every key bushing, and of the checks on grand keys. The latter can be recovered with felt and soft leather without difficulty if need be. If the grand keys' damper felts are replaced, the same thickness of material should be used. All bushings must be tested on their pins, remembering that the object is to achieve a free, but smooth and silent movement. If a key on the balance sticks one way or the other, you have to decide whether the centre or front bushing is at fault. If the cloth is not worn, the bushing can be loosened slightly by pressing between flat-nosed pliers, warmed if necessary (but not enough to char the bushing). If the bushing is compressed or even worn through (as is not uncommon) it will have to be replaced. Remove the old bushing by steam (a kettle will do), but hold over the steam no longer than necessary, since you do not want the wood swollen. Pry the bushing out once it is soft.

In replacing a centre bushing it is possible to work with the chase still in place, but there is a great likelihood that the glue will go in the wrong places. It is better to raise the chase with a knife and take it off, having softened its glue with vinegar. For the square top to this hole and for the front hole it is worth making a wooden plug which will fit loosely in the hole and help you to press the cloth firmly into place there, after which the edges are trimmed (Fig. 47).

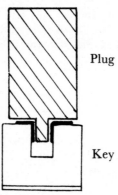

Plug

Key

Fig. 47. Key bushing plug

There should be hardly any movement possible sideways on the front rail. You may please yourself whether you re-bush, or merely turn the oval pin; the latter will eventually cause more wear but is of course a quick solution if the bushing has not disintegrated. The centre hole should permit no movement to front or back at the key bottom. If it is too free, drill a tiny hole behind or in front of the hole and tap in a fine splint to push the wall forwards. If it is too tight – for example after you have steamed it, or if it has been very damp – you need with a very fine file, or even a fine twist drill used as a rasp, to enlarge it slightly sideways, but do not touch the front or back.

Examine the capstans and plug their holes if they are loose. Dowel capstans can rust on to their wires and may require a drop of freeing fluid. (This is petrol-based; do *not* use oil of any kind anywhere in the action or serious damage will be done.) Replace their felt caps if necessary. Replacement dollies can be made from dowel drilled at the top with four holes for the regulating tool, and threaded to take the fixing wire.

Key covers are rather a problem to the amateur and there is no simple solution. Even if he can obtain a full set of whites, he may not wish to fit them for the sake of one natural which has a cigarette burn on it. Moreover, they may well be too thick and entail a new position for the key-frame. Equally, a new modern cover will never fit into a scale of old ivories or celluloids. One can but scout around in search of suitable plastics

141

or make the acquaintance of a junk shop owner or piano restorer who may have old covers to spare. If you have to fit a
cover which is thicker than the rest, remember to remove wood
from the key, particularly the front, or you will have problems.
If the difference is not extreme, it is possible to file down the
underside of the key at the centre hole rather than to make the
more difficult adjustment on the top surface. A difference of
colour is objectionable, but an even slightly projecting key looks
worse and a projection at the front can give trouble with the
key-slip. Should any key be actually broken, it can be glued
together and strengthened with a slip of veneer down each side.
A slightly warped key can be steamed and clamped. A badly
warped key may have to be broken, worked on with sandpaper,
and glued together true. This is mostly likely to be necessary
on the extreme 'doglegs' found in some older uprights.

Laying

Laying the keyboard is arranging all the keys on the key-
frame in such a way that they are level when at rest, horizontal
when about half-way down, and all have the correct key-dip
(10 mm). You need a long straight-edge, dip gauge, sharp
gauge (Chapter 1), and felt and paper punchings.

Ignore the sharps for the moment and take three naturals,
one from each end and one from the middle. Place a thick
punching on each oval pin in the front rail. If you have not
replaced the balance rail felts, you will probably have to make
only minor adjustments to the key dip. If you have to put in
new punchings, first try one and ascertain that the key's wood
does not touch the rail itself at all – if it does, there will be a
strange knocking when the piano is played. If there is any doubt
about this, put in a card punching to raise the key slightly.
Measure the key's dip from its bottom to the front rail felt. If
it is more than 10 mm, either you have too much thickness on
the balance rail, or slack needs to be taken up with card and
paper washers on the front rail. Keep the key as low on the
balance pin as possible rather than building up great piles of
punchings on each rail. Lay your other two keys in the same
way. Place your straight-edge across the outside keys and see
that the middle key reaches the edge, and that both ends
of the edge are the same distance above frame or bench. You

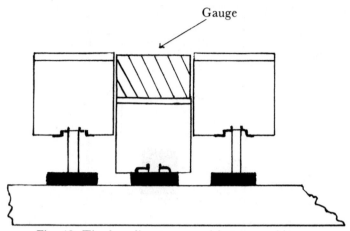

Fig. 48. The key-dip gauge used between whites

can then lay the rest of the keys with the straight edge as guide.

It is customary on the best pianos to have a slight upward bowing of the keyboard to the centre (where of course greater use will cause the keys to drop first), and you may be able to manage this with paper washers, but a really horizontal keyboard is satisfactory provided the keys are level. Always make sure that, whatever you may do during the laying, you end up with felt punchings on top, and paper or card washers underneath, or the latter will be audible. Do not bend the papers, or the folds will create temporary height which will soon be lost. Once you have established your guides, you use the straight-edge against the keys when they are at rest with their fronts up. The key-dip you set with your gauge by placing it on a depressed key and adjusting the front rail punchings until the top of the gauge is level with the top of the adjacent key when at rest (Fig. 48). You lay a forward – balanced keyboard in the same way as you lay a backward-balanced one, except that weights must be placed on the rear of its keys so that your norm for laying purposes is with the keys up. You will find that if you raise the level of a key by a washer on the balance rail, to make the key level, you are likely to have to make a corresponding adjustment on the front rail or the key-dip will be

143

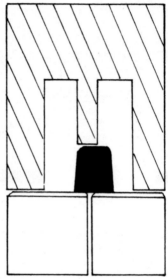

Fig. 49. The sharps height gauge

awry. Once you have all the white keys laid, you can proceed to the sharps employing similar methods and making use of your height gauge (Fig. 49).

Assembly and Strike-Line

Assume now that you have a properly laid keyboard ready to replace in the piano.

With a grand you should not have moved the stops which limit how far the key-frame can go back in, so you need merely screw the action back on, slide the frame back into the piano and check that the hammers do align with the strings. If you have moved the back stops you will find either that you cannot get the key-slip into position, or that the key-frame can be moved backwards so that there is a gap between the key fronts and the key-slip. Either state of affairs can be altered only by repeated further adjustment of the stops, and once that is done the strike-line for the hammers is bound to be as designed. If you choose to alter it you are probably spoiling the authenticity of the instrument and letting yourself in for some difficult cabinet-work.

144

With the upright it is less simple. If you have left the original shims in place in the key-bed, you can remove the necessary keys and screw down the key-frame, making sure that the shims are so placed that the frame is not subjected to any distorting tension by the screws. If you have thrown out the old shims, try various thicknesses until the key fronts are 2 mm below the top of the key-slip and with the slip not much more than 1 mm in front of them. Then adjust the shims so that they are clear of the screw-holes and use a spirit level to ensure that the frame is level from side to side and from front to back. This should result in a reasonable position for the keyboard although it may not be quite identical to the original site. If you now find that there is a gap between the capstans and the wippens you will know that you have fitted rather a thin back rail felt, have moved some of the capstans, or have the key-frame too low. Within limits these changes can be compensated for by adjustment of the capstans, which must be turned until the jacks in the action just touch the fronts of the notches in the hammer butts.

The 'strike-line' – that is, a hypothetical line across the strings where the hammer heads strike them – is critical to tone. In broad terms, the nearer to the middle a string is struck, the rounder is its tone. The nearer to the end it is struck, the brighter will be its tone. As we have seen, neither roundness nor brightness is inherently desirable. In a grand, the strike-line is unlikely to be altered, but in an upright it is possible for the action to drop and indeed it may be provided with adjustable foot screws. The line is a compromise, but it is based on the point required to sound the sixth partial (excluding the fundamental) of each string. This, for Middle C, corresponds to the Bb three octaves (less a note) higher. This partial is of course discordant with the fundamental C, being the first partial in the series which is so discordant. If the Middle C strings are struck at this point the partial fails to sound. Thus we require to strike a string at a point marking one-seventh of its speaking length. In practice, striking top notes at this point accentuates the mere thud of impact, and they are struck slightly higher, up to one-ninth. The covered strings are struck at nearer one-sixth, but the middle notes of the piano are struck at about one-seventh of their speaking length.

If the action drops, or if you have raised or lowered it, you will have affected the strike-line as it was intended and designed to be. That may not be the best possible strike-line for the instrument, but certainly the chances are that it will be. Therefore if, when you have replaced the key-frame, all the capstans need major adjustment — dowels may even screw off their wires or break because you screw them up or down too far — you must suspect that the action is high or low and the strike-line will be affected. You do not know the precise line for the instrument, but it is a fair assumption that the strike-point for Middle C will be at almost exactly one-seventh of the strings' speaking length. If you make that your mid-point and set the action with a spirit level, you will have good tone so far as strike-line is concerned. If, however, you seem to have perceptibily better tone on the top notes with the strike-line set higher, somewhere between one-seventh and one-eighth at Middle C, and you can adjust action and key-frame to this height without the keys coming over the key-slip, then this higher position may be worth adopting. (Remember that it is *speaking length*, not total length, with which we are concerned; you measure from the bridge pins to the agraffes or to the upper bearing beneath the pressure bar.)

146

Chapter Seven

TUNING, TONING AND HAMMER FELTS

TUNING

What is possible?

This chapter outlines some of the principles and indicates how you can make a start. Theoretically, piano tuning is a complex and somewhat mathematical subject. Practically, it depends enormously on experience. For fuller guidance on how to set about acquiring that experience there are several books in print – some of the older reprints are very helpful – and a selection of these is included in the Bibliography.

You may well wonder, if you have done nothing in this direction before, what is within your scope more or less immediately and on your own. The answer is that you can do much to improve the sound of a piano which, although professionally serviced, has been allowed to slide a bit, and you can bring a virtually pitchless piano into usable condition. It will be some time, however, before you can competently 'tune a piano', unless you devote a great deal of time and attention to study and practice. It is sensible for the owner and restorer to think in terms of 'touching up', making the instrument playable to his own standards – which will gradually rise – rather than of dispensing with the full attentions of the professional tuner on a regular basis, or to tune a piano which has been restored and brought to the stage at which it will hold its pitch but for which you are not quite sure if tuning or toning should be next in line. I believe that the beginner, at least, is being prudent, and is more likely to get satisfaction, if he has a piano professionally tuned before he attempts toning.

It is sometimes thought that various aids, particularly electronic, would put the piano tuner out of business if they were taken up by a discerning public. You have only to try using them to discover that this is not so. This is principally because they are in essence standard and mathematical, while every piano, even of the same model, is an individual instrument with

147

different harmonic characteristics from any other and suited to a particular range of tuning techniques. If you had a tuning fork for each of your 88 notes and successfully tuned the strings to the forks, the result would be at best dull – moreover, you would in fact find it very difficult to do. In the same way, if you have an electronic aid covering the whole range of the piano, you have to do more than turn the knobs and tuning pins to the appropriate positions. In addition, you have to acquire the knack of making the piano *stay* in tune, and that in itself takes more than one or two sessions.

Electronic aids vary. Some are merely accurate signal generators which will produce the theoretical pitch for every note on the piano. With these you have still to compare the vibrations of a string, and all its harmonics, with a pure electronically produced frequency, and that is not easy. Others will monitor the sound of a piano string and compare it with such an internal frequency standard, indicating the difference by means of an electronic eye or a needle on a scale. These, which are more expensive, obviously surmount a major difficulty, but still the comparison is with a standard, independently produced frequency and still the information is very difficult to apply in the top and bottom registers. It is in fact possible to arrange for such intruments to tune to partials rather than to fundamentals, and then you are indeed on the way. But there remains the wide area of subjective judgment where the trained ear will differ, for reasons which its owner knows, and the untrained ear will differ for reasons which its owner doesn't know, from what the machine indicates to be a true tuning. Therefore, although, if you propose to enter this pursuit on a considerable scale and are prepared to afford such an aid, it can be a great help to you, yet it will supplement rather than replace actual tuning experience. The more you tune, the more you will become aware both of its convenience and of its limitations, as indeed the more sensitive you will become to your piano's tuning – or temperament (the word is deliberately ambiguous).

There is no doubt – I speak with the certainty of experience – that to make one's first efforts with a tuning lever on a newly restrung piano of considerable age is a mistake, though an understandable one. A restrung piano will not hold its tuning for twenty-four hours and if the pins are loose it will never do so. Whilst you are tuning the top, the bottom goes out. The note against which you are tuning may itself by then be out of tune. So the excruciating unison which you discover may be a blunder on your part or may be due to settling of the strings or turning of the pins. In short, you have quite enough uncertainties with which to wrestle in your first steps in tuning, without adding to them huge uncertainties within the instrument.

I did eventually manage to tune my first restored piano after a fashion with a chromatic pitch pipe (after trying in vain to tune it to another, recently tuned, piano), and I persuaded it to stay in tune. But I would strongly urge anyone who has embarked on restoration to get the feel of a tuning lever and to get the required listening habit, before trying to tune an entirely pitchless and unstable instrument. He will be less put off and will form fewer bad habits, besides getting the restored piano better tuned. Using a tuned piano you can tune and untune unisons and octaves, and train yourself to listen to 'beats', without upsetting the piano tuner or breaking a string – these being the two disasters which spring to most's people's minds at the idea. You can, certainly, learn on any piano, but it is easier to pick up tuning on all but the smallest grand, rather than on an upright, especially if small. The notes sound for longer and the strings more nearly correspond to their theoretically required proportions.

Intervals and Beats

We shall have for a moment to return to the rather theoretical area in the early part of this book. We noticed then that – if the material and tension and thickness are constant – the lengths of strings are related in the same proportions as the frequencies of the sounds which their vibrations produce. For example, the C above Middle C (in these conditions) has a string half as long and vibrating twice as fast. The G (half an octave) above this has a string a third as long and vibrating three times as fast as that of Middle C (*see* Fig. 2). Obviously, however, the G just above Middle C must also be very closely related, since it is an exact octave below the G we have just mentioned. (In fact, Middle C is 2/3 of its frequency and their strings are related 3:2 in length.) C and G are the first two partials, the first notes of the harmonic series and (though it is in fact the top G) their intervals of an octave and a fifth are of special importance to the tuner.

It would be reasonable to infer from all this that every frequency is mathematically related to every other and every string proportionate. In fact, as we have seen, the strings cannot for practical reasons be proportionately long. Obviously, if we tuned every note with its octaves up the piano, we should soon run out of notes. After that, what we would need would be another note in a definite relationship to the first one, and the closest relationship is, of course, the fifth. Thus, if you used fifths and went both up and down, you would not run out of notes as you would with octaves. For example, you could go up from C to G, then another fifth to get D, go back an octave to the D and then tune up a fifth to A—and so on, coming back in the end to the first C. Although the strings cannot be strictly proportionate, the intervals of a fifth and an octave can easily be tuned by ear since they have the same 'clean' sound as a unison.

The tuner may well use such a method, in principle. But unfortunately he cannot use it in this simple form because the cycle of pure proportionate harmonic intervals in fact never adds up correctly. In other words, however accurate you tried to be, you would never come back to the first C. The note at which you arrived would be B sharp, and it would be sharp (by about a quarter of a semitone) of C as it has been established. This sharpness—known as the 'comma'—will occur no matter on what note you start if you proceed by the pure harmonic series. It follows that you must somehow distribute this discrepancy so that your cycle of fifths does bring you back to true C, and it is now established (though in some places only during this Century) that this shall be done by a system of 'equal temperament', dividing every octave into twelve equal semitone intervals. The consequence of this is that there are no pure harmonic intervals save the octave in the piano; a little distortion is added to every interval, though it is slight for the fifths. Mathematically, you could find the frequency of each note in the system by multiplying the preceding semitone by 1.0595; if you did this twelve times, you would arrive at exactly double the original frequency and so have the octave of the starting note.

The standard starting-point nowadays is A440—the A above

Middle C is to have 440 Hertz. But plainly, the tuner does not sit down with his calculator and equally certainly he does not start at the bottom and work up in semitones; if you try it, you will soon find that your notion of a semitone is a good deal hazier than you realized and it will be remarkable if after twelve attempts you come out at a pure octave of the starting note. Yet, if he does not primarily listen to intervals, to what does the tuner listen?

When we think of an instrument being 'in tune' or 'out of tune' we tend to think automatically of *pitch* and relative pitch (i.e. intervals). The tuner has acquired the habit of listening in a way which, while interesting, is not primary to a performing musician. He *hears* the total sound, the tone and pitch of the note at its greatest amplitude, but what he *studies* is the character of its decay, for in the decay of two notes he may hear 'beats', which are a far more accurate guide to the relationship of two pitches than is a sense of their fundamental vibration.

Some Experiments

Beats are the product of different frequencies. Sound waves consist of alternative compressions and rarefactions of air, as we have seen. If you superimpose two series of waves they will, according to their different lengths or frequencies, periodically combine and cancel each other out and, as both waves are quite regular, the result is a new vibration, of much slower frequency, coming and going, in other words a 'beat'. The frequency of the beat is in fact the difference between the fundamental frequencies. In practice beats become audible when a unison is imperfect or when two frequencies slightly fail to have an integral harmonic relationship to each other; and of course it is introducing a controlled type of such failure that constitutes equal temperament. If you depress and hold down adjacent notes on a piano you will in all probability not hear any beat, however acutely you listen to their decay. This is because, at most frequency levels, the beats of a whole semitone are too frequent for you to register them. Beats become slower as two wavelenths approach unity – this is of important practical use in tuning – but the higher you go up the scale in pitch, the more cycles per second (Hertz) there are between notes; the difference between Middle C and the next C sharp is 16 Hertz, which in terms of beats is still fast. More than about ten beats a second becomes a continuum of sound rather than a discernible beat. It is true that the lowest note in a piano vibrates at about 27 Hertz and a semitone above it is 29 Hertz, so you would have thought beats between adjacent semitones in the bottom bass would be distinctly audible. But on a piano this is unfortunately not so, for a reason noted earlier – the extreme lack of clarity of the fundamental frequencies in the bass notes.

For the moment, therefore, you will do better deliberately to create beats from intervals less than a semitone. This you can most easily do by taking two strings which ought to vibrate without beats and adjusting one of them so that it vibrates sharp or flat, but by much less than a semitone. Alternatively, you can use another instrument – an electronic organ is particularly suitable – with a clearer fundamental frequency in the bass, and listen to the throbbing beats of adjacent notes; they are strongly audible with the 16 foot stop on an organ. On the piano use the middle range – say Middle C again – and silence one of the three strings with a felt or rubber mute. Then apply the tuning lever to one or other of the two strings and very slightly turn it – do be careful that it is the pin of one of the strings to which you are listening that you turn. Do little more than try to bend the lever, turning anti-clockwise to flatten the string. Play the note repeatedly, holding the key down each time as you listen to the decay, and you should hear the beats. Plate 15a is an oscillogram of fast beats in a second produced this way – 15b shows the detail on a faster time-base. Turn the lever more, and the throbs will grow more rapid until you are hearing two distinct sounds rather than one sound with a beat. If you now start to restore the tuning, you will be carrying out a fundamental tuning process – tuning a unison; you turn the pin until you can hear no more beats – the unison is clean and pure. You may, of course, go too far, when the beats will be heard again and you must turn the lever back till they disappear. In fact, you should go a little too far – more a matter of tension in the handle and pin than of actual rotation – or the string will go flat soon after you take the lever off and certainly when the note is played.

In a piano, therefore, the two or three strings of a unison are beatless. You soon come to sense the 'quiet', 'clear' quality

152

of a perfect unison. The same is true of octaves. Mute a pair of a trichord, and then a pair of the trichord an octave above, and repeat the same experiment using one string in each trichord. Do not listen for the pitch, but for the quietness, the freedom of beats, of the strings. Of course, there may not be such a freedom. In that case, the piano is out of tune. If it sounded in tune to you, most probably a pair of strings in each octave was beatless, but two strings were not. It is most likely the upper trichord which is 'out' and you can go on to test the unison of these three strings, and of the three lower ones, and adjust matters so that all strings of the same pitch are in unison and also beatless with strings at an octave's distance.

It is worth exploring the unisons of the piano to give you experience in handling the lever and in listening to beats. Do not be afraid that in doing this you will break a string or incur the displeasure of your tuner. By these slight movements you will not break a string unless the piano has been untuned for years and there is rust forming; but always take the precaution of letting a string go slightly flat before increasing its tension. So far as the tuner is concerned, at first do not alter the pitch of every string in a trichord or bichord. Then you can always restore the tuning to its original condition, poor as that may have been, by tuning the unisons back to the untouched strings. It is far more likely, however, that you will find it worthwhile to have a chat with the tuner and that you will pick up some hints from it.

After the first experiments with unisons and octaves, test strings against their octaves to ascertain which are the most likely to be correct and which have strayed, and try to polish up the unisons throughout. Then go on to fifths. If the piano is in tune, these intervals will shows beats of around one a second in the middle of the piano. Try moving the pin so that the interval ceases to beat – a 'perfect fifth' – and then turn it back to the previous position, as still held by the rest of the trichord. Become familiar with the sound of a beatless fifth and of beats gradually added to it.

You will notice that, as you go up the piano, increasingly small movements of the tuning lever produce increasingly large effects until, at the very top, you seem scarcely to move the pins, but rather to twist them slightly to alter the tension. In fact, if the pins are tight, this happens anywhere in the scale. When you apply your lever you create or reverse torsion in the pin and this must minutely affect pitch although, owing to the larger wavelengths, it is less noticeable lower down the piano. This is put to use in 'setting' the pin to stay in tune.

It is essential for the string to exert pressure – 'down-bearing' – on the bridge if the vibrations are to be transmitted to the soundboard. Furthermore, to secure this and a clean start to its speaking length, it is forced beneath a pressure bar and over (or under) an upper bearing, or through a stud screwed into the frame (Fig. 19). All this creates friction. When you turn a pin to tighten a string, the tension goes immediately into the short dead length between the pin and the upper bearing. Some of it then goes into the speaking length and some again into the dead length at the hitchpin, but the string will not stay in tune if you merely turn the pin and hope for the best, because when it is struck by the hammer the still uneven tension will gradually be equalized. Consequently, while it may have seemed in tune at the time, the tension of the whole string will become less as the strain is distributed into the speaking length. You must, therefore, try to have this distribution occur at the time of tuning, not during subsequent playing. This you do by striking the key quite hard and repeatedly whilst you are tuning the string, and you neutralize the torsion on the pin by edging it down very slightly after turning it up. The family will decide that you are unmusical and would do better to restrict your servicing to the car, but there really is no alternative to this mechanical striking of the keys when tuning a piano. The time for subtle variations of touch is in playing it or when testing the toning of the hammers.

Tuning

It will be apparent by now that much of the work of tuning is done by securing beatless unisons and octaves. But of course you cannot stop there, and what you need is an accurately tuned octave or so from which to derive the other notes. Such an octave is selected in the middle of the piano, because it is here that beats are most easily heard, and tuning it is known as 'laying the bearings'.

For the moment, you can lay the bearings by various aids,

of which the octave chromatic pitch pipe, a one-octave accurately-tuned electronic organ, or a larger scale signal generator or tuning aid are the simplest. With these – save for the 'visual display' tuning aids, where of course you rely on the meter or optical indicator – you proceed note by note, trying by listening to secure accurate unisons between the string and the aid. You tune only one string of a group at the same time; silence the other two at each note with a mute between them, or with a continuous strip of felt pried between the relevant pairs of strings. The advantage of the strip-mute is that it obviates confusing vibrations from strings of different pitch. The reason for tuning single strings is that the unisons are a complication. If they are at all less than perfect, they will be difficult to tune to, and the more you can concentrate on just two strings (or one string) at a time, the better. (Another reason, if the piano is below pitch, is that this method spreads the increase in tension over an area.)

Your basic pitch you will have to establish, say to A440, with a tuning-fork of this frequency. If you use an electronic device this will probably have to be adjusted to the tuning-fork's frequency first of all. If you do not use such a device or other aid, you will have to listen very accutely to beats, because the quarter of a semitone which has to be distributed over an octave, as already mentioned, is distributed by tuning perfect intervals sharp or flat by a certain number of beats per second. This timing of beats eventually becomes a second sense. It can, in theory, be measured on the job with the beat of a grandfather clock (one a second) or a metronome (set to 60 – one click a second) as background – visual check from the seconds hand of a clock or watch will not be found very helpful. In practice this is not as simple as it may seem since, even in the middle of the piano, the sustaining time which is really audible is not great. We are concerned with beats of ± 1 per second. One string of A440 with the key held down will not be usefully audible for much more than ten seconds on a good piano – considerably less for tuning purposes in ordinary surroundings. If you are not too sure what you are doing anyway, that is not long to detect the beat and then to measure how often it occurs. So it is simplest to use a rule of thumb, noting whether or not you can hear two or three distinct beats when the note

155

has been struck firmly, but not violently, before the sound fades.

How do we use our experience of beats in laying the bearings without a tuning aid? There are many ways, and also many ways of checking the results when the job is done, but we will settle for the simplest – which in essence has already been noted. This depends on using a cycle of fifths, appropriately adjusted, until we come back to the starting point and, hopefully, find unison with our first string there. Only the octave and the unison are free of beats in the equal tempered system, so we must tune every fifth until it beats at a rate appropriate to its place on the full scale of frequencies. In the middle of the piano, this is about three beats in five seconds, and you can take this as being two clearly audible beats before the sound goes. To be more accurate, you can set your metronome to 72 and expect to hear one beat for every two clicks that it makes. Bear in mind the sound of a perfect fifth from your earlier experiments – it is one of the most familiar of intervals.

Your procedure is to tune perfect fifths, as you would unisons or octaves, and then to distune them until you hear the required beats. So long as you are tuning upwards from a lower note, you make the fifths *flat* to the extent of two beats. By this method you will never in fact have to tune down except for an octave; this you do whenever it will bring you nearer to your goal (A440) again. So start by tuning A an octave below A440; then a fifth above that (E); then a fifth above that (B), when you drop an octave to the lower B. You will run into some complicated accidentals (F double-sharp, etc.) towards the end, but do not worry about this. In fact, there is no need to work it out on paper – just remember that for a fifth there must be six hammers between the two whose strings you are tuning. It will take you twelve steps to get back to the original A – whose notation will be G double-sharp. As you go up, tune to a beat-rate gradually on the fast side; the beat-rate for a fifth doubles in speed in the course of an octave. This, apart from the difficulty of hearing fast beats, is the reason why you lay the bearings within as small a pitch-range as possible.

There are other, more sensitive, ways of laying the bearings, and in particular in due course you will need to be familiar with the beat-rates of other intervals at various points on the

156

scale, because these are used for tests and checking that all is well. But this is a reasonable and logical way in which to start. It can be used particularly when an instrument has been restrung or at least has had all tension removed, and you must start from scratch. By that time you will have done so much already that you will wish to pick up the sense of tuning and make the piano playable, rather than enter a full study of the science and practice of the art.

When you have laid the bearings, you continue with tuning, or put the unisons in at this stage. At least if the instrument is being tuned virtually 'from scratch' and there is doubt as to how it will hold, it is best to tune one string throughout before putting in unisons. In tuning the rest of the piano, you go basically by octaves from the laid bearings, taking sample intervals for test as you go. Here your ear is a very much better guide to you than most tuning aids. This is partly because, with the top strings, a small movement of the pin will send the visual aid right off the chart and, with the bottom strings, the fundamental is difficult to pick up anyway. But it is also because (as we have seen) all pianos have a degree of 'inharmonicity', which is greater on small pianos and high notes, but also present in low notes because of their mass and relative stiffness. 'Inharmonicity' – a word so horrible as almost to suggest its meaning – is a deviation of fundamentals from their harmonic equivalents; each fundamental, each note, is of course a partial for many other fundamentals, but its sound as a partial may not be identical in pitch with its sound as a fundamental although it would be if the true mathematical proportion of string lengths could be followed throughout. The further we go up the piano (and the further down, but it is most noticeable at the top), the greater does this deviation become. Thus the first partial of a string is likely to sound sharp of the string's true octave at double its frequency. Moreover, this apparent sound is more important to the listener than any theoretical wavelength for the upper note. Thus the octave note ought to be in tune with the audible partial of the string an octave below.

Thus the theoretical octaves have to be 'stretched' – tuned increasingly on the sharp side. It is important to say that if you tune the octaves, by ear, so that they are beatless, you will automatically make this adjustment, though you need a sense, referring to pitch rather than beats, that the octaves are at least 'not sounding flat'. If you use a machine, you will not make the adjustment unless you do so deliberately, and some aids do give you directions on how to tune to the lower note's harmonic. Remember, especially if you are tuning by ear entirely, that the beats of notes at the top of the piano are fast and not easy to hear, and the notes do not sound for very long at all. Consequently, it is common to tune progressively sharp because it is recognized that the ear tends to hear a top note flat although in fact it is strictly in tune. Here a good sense of pitch, rather than of beats, comes into its own.

The degree of 'stretching' depends on particular pianos and particular tuners. It is a matter of taste which you have gradually to settle for yourself. It is easiest not to restrict yourself to comparing one note with its immediate octave, but to play four or five ascending octaves and to judge if the last one falls short. The bass strings similarly are adjusted, being made slightly flat towards the bottom, but this is a good deal less critical to the ear since they are apt to sound uncertain in pitch anyway. Of course, having been warned of the need for 'stretching', do not overdo it – for this is the inevitable tendency.

There are difficulties, some already mentioned, in tuning the very top and the very bottom strings, and there are two little hints which can help. The first, for top notes, is to include plucking individual strings in your repertoire; while it is possible to be misled by the different tone of a finger-nail from a felt hammer, this can be helpful with top unisons. Secondly, with bass strings, try touching a monochord at a half or a third of its speaking length and tuning that to the string an octave, or an octave and a fifth, above; frequently the first and second partials are clearer than the fundamentals, and if you tune one you will automatically tune the other.

Raising Pitch

It is most unlikely that any iron-framed or iron-braced piano which you come across cannot be tuned to A440, concert pitch. Unless it is cracked, the frame will stand the tension. Whether the strings or bridges or wrestplank will do so is another matter, but reasonable judgment is possible from the general condition of these parts. If, so far as you know, the piano has long been below pitch (and this means a semitone or more overall), you must not try to bring it up before checking the condition of these items and repairing as necessary. If strings break, they were due for replacement anyway. However, raising pitch often takes some time and always involves a great increase in internal stresses. If an elderly instrument is well set below pitch – i.e. it is staying in tune but is flat overall – there is much to be said for leaving well alone unless, of course, it is essential to bring it up to pitch because it is to be used with other instruments of set pitch higher than its own; whether the human voice is such an instrument obviously depends on the singer ...

If you decide to go forward, it is asking for trouble to raise the pitch more than a semitone *in one go*. Start with the bass, where the frame is more massive, and raise each note and its octaves in turn, thus spreading the strain – if necessary, first tune the piano thoroughly to its present pitch, taking Middle C or the A above as your starting point. If you have more than a semitone to go in all, tune each (new) note to the (old) note a semitone above it. Raise the whole to about a semitone below concert pitch and then leave it for a day or two to settle down – a similar procedure can be followed after re-stringing, but then start with the whole about an octave flat. Then you can make the further increase, if possible tuning the middle range very slightly sharp and not stretching the octaves at this stage. Leave it again and only at the third attempt think you are working towards a more permanent tuning. If the instrument is re-strung, you will need to tune it at least five times before stability begins to become apparent.

TONING AND HAMMER FELTS

The hammer felts are, with the bridges and soundboard, perhaps the most dangerous areas in the piano; their condition is vital to the instrument's performance, but damage done here by injudicious meddling may well be irreversible.

Re-covering and Reshaping (Plate 10)

The only satisfactory way for hammers to be recovered is professionally, by machine. Here graded and shaped felt can be applied at such pressure that the desirable compression at the centre, and tension at the outside of the covering is assured. Equally, you will have a series of properly weighted and shaped hammers. However, there are other steps that may be taken subject to the condition of the hammers and the value of the piano.

The first alternative is hand-covering with true hammer felt made for this purpose. This comes in tapered sheets and your guide as to size is the thickest unworn portion of the lowest hammer in your piano — go by the sides, not the face, which will be compressed. Do not buy thicker felt out of a feeling that a heavier hammer will produce better tone. Probably it will not. It will adversely affect the touch and whole action and you will find that the taper overall is incorrect, so that the thinnest felt is too thick for your treble hammers unless filed down in an arbitrary fashion. The thickness here is far more critical than it is in the bass and too thick felt will result in a dead treble register.

The machine covers the hammers in a block and then separates them, but you will have to see to each one individually. In removing the old felts, cut straight down the strike points and peel off the felts in halves. Any underfelt may be left intact. Take great pains to have the new felt strips of exactly the same width, and to trim the back edges off at consistent angles and in a dead straight line — this does a great deal for appearance. Cut the ends to a taper (Plate 10) against the sides of the head before sticking. When sticking, cramp the hammer and those ends in a vice or clamp; that way the felt is stretched tightly round the striking point and shoulders. A strong impact adhesive is suitable. Stop at the shoulders — never let adhesive come near the strike points. When the new felts are on, they will be found, by the tension involved, to present a concave striking surface towards the strings. This must of course be rectified with the sand-file. First file the sides of the hammers so that wood and felt are completely level, then file the edges so as to give the merest hint of a convex surface (Fig. 50). Do not file what will be the striking surface; the pressure of hand-covered felt is already weak without the additional problem of making the strike point soft and fluffy. If the treble hammers are too soft when you come to try them, harden them by ironing towards the strike point, the heat discolouring the felt very

160

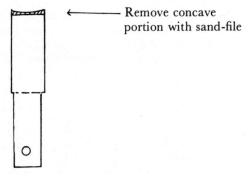

Fig. 50. Shaping new hand-covered hammer felts

slightly. File the scorched felt off lightly with a fine file. In my experience doping the hammer with lacquer to harden the surface, though it has been recommended, produces a quite unacceptable tone.

The second alternative, to be preferred to hand-covering unless the hammers are in really desperate straits, is to reshape and repair them. This is only possible where there is some meat left on the hammers at the strike-point, although where a treble hammer has worn right through it is possible to repair with kid or chamois leather stretched tightly. Reshaping is done with sand-files, starting with a medium grade and working down through finer grades. If the felt is very yellow or dirty, rub in white or cream tailor's chalk to restore the colour, before you apply the file, and brush out the chalk later. Although the wear is on the strike-point, it is not from here that you remove felt; you file along the sides towards the strike-point, as if to push the felt over it afresh, and then tone the compressed strike-point as necessary. Work from the sides alternately till there is a loose knop over the strike point, and then gently brush this until it goes. Removing trenches by filing down the strike-point will simply bring the demise of the hammer that much nearer. The strike-point *is* a point, a narrow line across the face; it is not a flattened surface. It may not be easy to detect on a well-furrowed hammer. Assume it to lie in a straight line from the centre of the wood, or find its location with the hammer in the piano, and mark the line in pencil so that you know what you are working towards (Fig. 51, Plate 10). The hammers must

161

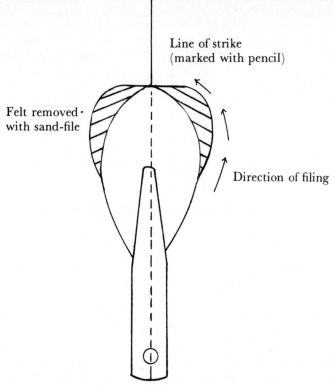

Line of strike
(marked with pencil)

Felt removed·
with sand-file

Direction of filing

Fig. 51. Shaping worn hammer felts

be filed symmetrically so that there is equal weight above and
below the strike-point. The strike-point, which corresponds to
the strike-line on the strings, must not be moved since, as we
have seen, where the string is struck governs the tone. When
sanding, it is not necessary to remove all the scoring by the
strings – it will anyway soon reappear – but you must try to
obtain a rounded point, rather than a large area of the hammer,
striking the strings, and the grooves made by the strings will
need decompressing by toning.

Toning

In Plate 5 are shown wave characteristics of strings struck
by hammers in different conditions. Where the hammer is hard
and worn, there is a profusion of partials, giving a very involved
picture. This sound is harsh and hard, with a noisy onset. Where
the felt is soft the amplitude or volume is low and the partials

162

are relatively few. This sound is dull and mushy. We require something in between – a tense and elastic layer and a compressed interior to the felt. This is secured by toning.

Toning is the insertion of needles into the felt to lessen its compaction. Obviously, therefore, toning can do nothing for a hammer which is too soft – and in fact hammers only become too soft as a result of excessive and imprudent toning, presenting a condition which can never be well remedied. It is a fairly easy matter to pick about in the striking surface of a hammer so that you have a pleasant mellow tone when the piano is played quietly, but in the first place pianos are not always played quietly, and in the second place such a softening will not last very long. In fact you must tone hammers for the whole range of playing and, throughout the piano, this takes a long time – though often all that is required is the correcting of certain notes which stand out as too bright among the rest (Fig. 52).

For loud toning, the operative part of the felt is the bulging shoulder and you insert a strong needle deeply several times on either side of the hammer at that point, observing the effect as you do so, and using a constant, almost mechanical, touch. It is normal to insert needles radially, but for more drastic cases it is possible to insert from the rear of the hammer. Never insert sideways, for this layers the felt. Your needles should go deep, but not so deep as to meet the wood.

For medium toning you use a finer needle and repeat the process on either side of the strike-point, i.e. at about eleven and one o'clock if you hold the hammer with the tail at six o'clock. For soft toning you approach the striking area with finer needles still and this, now you have voiced more deeply, will have more lasting effect.

Toning depends partly on your ear and aural memory and partly on feel. You have to remember, as you move up or down the piano, what a previous note sounded like and try to introduce a compatible tone into the one which you are treating. It is all too easy to make each note a bit softer than the one before, then to go back and soften that one to match. You end up with an uninteresting mush, and nothing can restore those felts to their ideal condition. The best thing is ironing them, pressing them towards the crown as you do so, with an iron

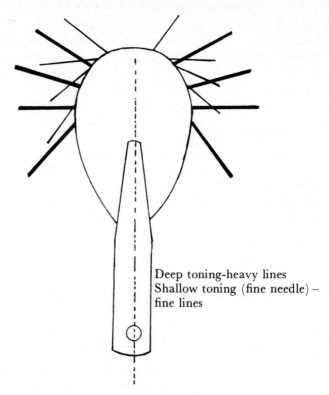

Deep toning-heavy lines
Shallow toning (fine needle) –
fine lines

Fig. 52. Toning hammer felts

just below charring heat. As has been said, this may also be necessary with the top treble of newly hand-covered felts, which are inclined to turn out too soft. But of course ironing is no substitute for the tension which is really required and it is far better to avoid the need for it. A domestic iron is rather unwieldy but quite satisfactory for ironing felts.

Toning can be done with the action in the piano, using a board to keep fluff out of the works. In fact, it should be done so, because you must be able to hear what sound you are creating. With a grand, it is easiest to sit at the piano and slide the action out – watching those hammer shanks against the wrest-plank! – so that it balances on one's lap and the key-bed. Do not be in a hurry to tone. In particular, never consider toning until a piano has settled down well in tune. It is quite fruitless to try to eliminate beats and undesirable partials by toning the hammers when in fact the trouble is in the strings. It will be obvious to you if a whole instrument is out of tune. If it is odd notes that bother, then it is not difficult to check their tuning before taking irreversible steps with the hammers.

Chapter Eight

GENERAL POINTS ON BUYING AND RESTORATION

In this chapter we shall consider more broadly how to assess a piano's condition, what you can do to improve it, and the chances of buying a piano which it would be worth your while to try to restore. Notes on repairing the various parts of a piano have been given, but there remains the question of how far to go and in what sequence to approach a thorough overhaul. It is assumed that you know whether you want an upright or a grand, or already have one or the other. There are probably more bargains to be had in the way of grands, and you should end up with a better instrument, but against this has to be set the much greater requirement for space and the considerably larger manual task of restoration if you tackle a grand.

BUYING AN OLD PIANO

Types

If you buy or otherwise come by an old piano which you hope to restore, it is prudent to ensure if possible that it is of a type which will eventually be resaleable. You are quite likely in due course to want to exercise your skills on a better instrument, and you will almost certainly improve your musical judgment to the extent that you will require a better instrument than your first to play. Pianos occupy space, gather dust, require servicing and are heavy. Only a few people are prepared to collect them or to adopt and restore models of historic interest, and the latter is a specialist subject outside the scope of this book. Similarly, it is wise to avoid a compass of less than seven octaves, because a small compass means a reduced market.

You can learn a great deal from an overdamped upright, as from an upright or grand which is straight strung, but (unless you require a piece of special interest) such pianos are generally difficult to sell save for a sum less than the cost of the piano, materials and tools to you. (We will assume you do not cost your time as well.) They can of course be acquired for nominal sums, especially if you can transport them, but they will eventually be hard to dispose of. Therefore for practical purposes, and despite higher initial prices, it is best to stick to overstrung pianos with iron frames. Uprights should generally be under-damped and it is preferable, but not essential, that grands have repetition actions. Sources vary from inheritance or gift, to specialist dealers (who, particularly in the London and Birmingham areas, often 'turn round' cheap pianos as an alternative to exporting them by the load) and advertisements in local newspapers and *Exchange and Mart*.

Condition

Pianos are often sold as 'needs tuning' or 'musician's instrument'. These and similar phrases may mean about as little as the jargon of estate agents about compact bedrooms and sought-after areas. A true 'musician's instrument' can have had a very hard life indeed and be superseded as no longer servicable even for unmusical pupils. It may be a bit like the vaunted car of a 'sales executive' – well run in. If it is really such that only a true 'musician' can discern its outstanding merits, one must wonder why it is not advertised in the *Musical Times* or National Press or has not been snapped up by a dealer. A 'learner's piano' is by implication one which no self-respecting pianist would dream of playing in its present condition – and it is therefore also totally unsuited to a learner, who should have the benefit of a decent instrument. On the other hand, a 'learner piano' may be sound but tatty – a good subject for renovation. 'Needs tuning' may mean that more than tuning is needed. If the piano is so badly out of tune that the owner draws attention to the fact, the chances are that it will not stay in tune for any period because of the poor condition of the wrestplank. You may or may not be able to improve matters, but you should be aware of what you are taking on.

Contrary to what one might think in a sophisticated way, the state of a piano's case can be some guide as to the state of the instrument and the surroundings in which it has been. Missing music desks, damaged pedals and screwed down panels suggest a church hall or pub piano, which will probably have been ill-maintained and subject to vandalism. Unlike a car, a piano's exterior is not often 'tarted up' for sale, since the sale price of old pianos is so low that it would not be worth the expense – the exception being the 'famous name' which will command money, almost regardless of condition, but will command still more if made a presentable instrument and piece of furniture. However, it is as well to remember that to give a piano a 'name' – especially if the sign already begins with 'Stein ...' but does not end in '-way' – is a very simple matter indeed. 'Name' pianos are as subject to age and decay as others; by the time you have replaced the strings and most of the felts there may not be anything very distinctive about one and it is a mistake to pay much over the odds for a retired *piano* just because it originated in a famous stable.

Pianos in which moth and rust and worm have been extensively at work may be better avoided. It depends what you are prepared to do. Such instruments have in all probability to be completely re-strung and re-felted in both action and keyboard. This is a long and costly undertaking if the eventual quality of the instrument will still be doubtful.

What you need, if you are contemplating an instrument to restore for personal use and pride, is a piano which has been played, and serviced after a fashion, not totally neglected by player and tuner, nor beaten to death by players and non-players alike. It may or may not have suffered from central heating, but it will not have spent years in the garage absorbing dampness whose drying out will create all manner of complaints. You may have to re-string it and do a good many repairs throughout, but you may not have to replace every single bushing, centre and spring in the action. You expect to find wear and even damage on the case where it has been handled and moved – on the desk, round the fall, around the pedals and bottom board, discoloured keys and faded felts and braids. The strings, whilst not heavily rusted, may well appear polished where they have been covered by hammers and dampers, but be otherwise dull. The tuning pins will not be badly rusted, but they may be superficially brown and be a bit mauled from a tuning lever. The hammers might be well worn, but there would remain meat on them for reshaping, as they have not been much reshaped before. If occasional hammer shanks have broken – usually owing to excessively dry conditions, or to rough handling of a grand action – the heads may well be found somewhere in the case. A few keys may rub, but a keyboard that jams solid in several places may be better avoided because almost certainly the key balance holes are worn even beyond the bushings. Likewise, worn bushings on the grand's damper guide rail are to be expected, but you may baulk at remaking every one of them. You have to judge whether you will be able to cope with missing or chipped key covers; imperfect key coverings tend to have an effect on resale prospects which is quite disproportionate to their intrinsically small importance.

It is as well to inquire as to tuning history. A piano tuned recently may well not hold its pitch – it may have been tuned for sale. Aside from the need for space and the absence of a player, inability of a piano to hold its pitch must be one of the commonest reasons for disposing of it and you should keep this in mind. A piano very badly below pitch and out of tune is a risky buy. The best bet is an instrument which is reasonably in tune but which has not just been tuned. If the pins then turn out to be loose from place to place, they can probably be tightened. One has to go by inference and inquiry, because it is unlikely to be possible to test the tightness of the pins when one is considering purchase.

As has already been indicated, it is most unwise to buy a piano, however tempting, with a cracked frame – whatever the owner says about 'having it welded'. Cracks are usually by the bars in the area of the tuning pins and easily visible. A superficial crack here is as serious as a clear break which will probably follow once you dismantle. You cannot repair such a frame and it will be very difficult to get anyone to take the job on, for such repairs do not last. In its present state, you can have no knowledge of how long the frame will continue to support the full tension or of how long it is all held together by the wrestplank below – which may also be cracked. Such a piano is a liability, unless you buy it purely for spare parts.

Cracked soundboards are another matter. Whether they are to be avoided will depend on how bad the cracks are and where they are. It is the cracks – actually split joints – between sound-board planks which are serious, and they are normally accompanied by loose bars and warping. Repair may well be possible, but it will involve removal of the frame and stringing and you have to decide whether you want to go this far. Likewise with cracks in the bridges on the line of the pins. Superficial openings round the pins are common and even normal. Short or intermittent deeper cracks can be repaired if the associated strings are removed. But a bridge split right the way along, with loose and crooked pins, is a very different proposition. To examine the soundboard, you will need to remove top and bottom panels of an upright, and if possible the action. In a grand, bridges and soundboard are more visible once the top is lifted. A torch shone behind an upright or under a grand is helpful in assessing the soundboard's condition.

It is safe to assume that any piano more than fifty years old will need re-stringing whatever use it has had (unless, of course, it is known to have been re-strung before) and it is almost certain that its soundboard will have sunk a certain amount. If the soundboard is not actually damaged (or is repairable) and re-stringing can be undertaken, however, it ought to be possible to bring the instrument up to pitch and to obtain a pianistic tone from it. Whether it will be economic to do this restoration is another matter. The cost of wire, felt and miscellaneous materials will set you back considerably, although you will probably not add the cost of your time. The latter is, of course, the great saving. Therefore the total bill may well be much less than you would pay for a professionally restored instrument of similar vintage; and you will have had a great deal of pleasure on the way.

Age

It is not necessarily important to know the precise age of a piano. If you wish to do so, you may be able to establish it from the serial number on case, frame and soundboard – these numbers (not all of which may be present) should agree, whilst any number on the action may well not agree – and reference to the books mentioned in the Bibliography. The style and finish of the case and type of frame and action also all tell a story. But the exact date of the piano is of much less importance to you than its present condition and the treatment it has had. If it is more than thirty years old the downbearings are likely to be a little reduced, the strings to be fatigued, and the hammer felts to be hard and discoloured. These faults do not make a piano beyond redemption, but they do make many pianos barely economic propositions save for the amateur. What you may ideally want to find (according to time and materials available) is a piano with little else seriously wrong with it, when you can be fairly sure that you will eventually produce a restored instrument which is satisfying to play and looks not far off new save in style. Pianos ready for such treatment are not sought after very widely, being a little too far gone for straight second-hand purchase, and they can be very cheap. Provided that you are able to avoid buying more trouble than you in your circumstances can cope with, you have a very good chance of picking up a bargain and of finding pleasure in bringing out its true potential.

Price

Prices of old pianos vary very widely indeed. By and large, dealers offer vendors very low prices because of the high cost of restoration – principally the cost of skilled craftsmen's time – and because the rebuilt piano, unless with a famous name, must be sold at a price substantially below that of a new model with reasonable appeal. The cost of restoration may well add 100 per cent to the price which a dealer gives. Despite inflation, the price of new pianos is not beyond the reach of home pianists and, particularly for those who are not serious musicians, their attraction in terms of size and as fashionable furniture is very much greater than the attraction of older and larger (musically often preferable) instruments. Even in part-exchange one may be offered for an old piano little but the price of removal to a scrapyard.

So people try the open market by means of advertisement, pricing sometimes outrageously highly and sometimes asking little more than the cost of getting the unwieldy and unwanted object out of the house. Sometimes a seller believes he has inherited an object of musical interest and prices it accordingly as if it were a desirable antique. But in this field the market for standard antiques of their day is very small indeed and the great majority of nineteenth century – even early nineteenth

171

century – pianos are not sold to collectors or restored, but destroyed, save for their timber which is recycled.

Since prices are so chaotic, the private sale has to be approached with some caution. Bargains mingle with rubbish, prices having little rationale, and it pays to look around. It may also pay to be wary of advertisers who will arrange transport, for this can be the despairing bid of someone anxious to offload a white elephant, and applies to dealers as well as individuals. However, obviously transport is a problem and may sensibly make a contribution to price.

Moving a Piano

The piano has come to your door and you have to get it inside or to a work area. Observe how it is handled by the removal men, if it is, for they have a knack – though you will need more people, probably two for an upright and at least three for a grand.

The upright you lift as little as possible. Find a secure part of the bottom board and get the trolley underneath it. Failing this, check that the action is secure, turn the piano on its side, and then use the trolley. If you have no trolley, put as little strain on the castors as you can. Remember that the weight is in the frame, at the back. Removing parts – for example, panels, fall and action – will make little difference to the total weight and awkwardness. Even old uprights with wide keybeds will usually go through a standard sized internal door. There will probably be a bar at the back, on older pianos, level with the keybed, whilst on modern pianos there are usually handholds at this height. Lift by bar or handhold at the back and by key-bed at the front as far as possible.

With a grand, make sure that the action is securely wedged beneath the front of the frame – sometimes there is a screw for the purpose. Alternatively, take out the action; since the keyboard is attached, this does significantly reduce the piano's weight. Take off the fall, hinged top and music desk – they also affect weight, whilst the desk and fall may drop off, and be damaged if not removed. The piano has then to be lifted and held raised whilst someone unscrews the legs and it is moved on to the trolley, which should go under the straight side. The width of grands does not, of course, vary much and neither does their depth, so that subject to any tight bends the piano can be pushed around on its straight side. A piano that has been transported, with however few hitches, will need tuning, and possibly re-tuning, if playing is envisaged at this stage.

RESTORATION

Planning the Work

The work of restoring a piano, upright or grand, falls naturally into several sections and, because of problems of access, some of these can only be tackled in a certain order. Broadly, these sections are the action, the keyboard, stringing and frame, soundboard and bridges, and the case. Some work can be carried on whilst other work is taking its time. For example, you can be occupied on action and keyboard whilst the case or frame is drying or whilst replaced strings are brought gradually nearer pitch. Equally, you cannot regulate the action properly until the strings have been reinstated and you cannot tone the hammers until the whole piano is assembled, tuned and settled. Therefore you need to take stock of the situation and to work out a plan of campaign, subject as this may be to nasty discoveries like damage to the soundboard which has been concealed by the frame.

There are degrees of renovation. Tuning and regulation you can generally improve without new materials or much in the way of tools. With the upright you need do little more than remove the top and bottom doors and then get to work. To make small adjustments to a grand's action you may not need to make a regulating bar. However, regulation is much better carried on in full throughout, and for the grand you must anyway remove the action and take up a good deal of space before you can do anything at all.

You may then decide that strings, frame and soundboard are in order, but hammers need recovering or reshaping, dampers need refelting, respringing and regulating, and the keyboard needs regulation or relaying. This calls for a limited plan in which you make space for the action and key-frame, but leave the basic structure intact. Work on grand dampers is separate from work on the action and keyboard and should be done afterwards, in case small alterations to the keys affect the

173

dampers. On the other hand, extensive work on upright dampers has to be done with the action dismantled, though they can be regulated only after assembly. The upright or grand keyboard can be worked upon at any stage so long as the action is removed first.

If you have more extensive restoration in mind, you can leave the action and keyboard aside until later but, before stripping the structure down, remember to take essential measurements – of downbearing at several places along the bridges, of the height of the frame above the soundboard at various points, and of the height of any pressure bar. With uprights it is a wise precaution to measure also the height of the top of the piano above the hammer rail, and the height of the key-frame above the key-bed; these will serve as guides in replacing the action.

With uprights, you must remove the key-bed before you can take off the strings; it may be screwed up into the cheeks from below or it may be virtually solid with them or it may be fixed to them with oblique screws concealed beneath the key-frame. It is usual to remove and replace strings of an upright piano with the instrument on its back, though this is not essential. (For letting down and removal, *see* Chapter 3 – Repairs – Strings.) With grands, you must remove the dampers – and therefore also the action to be able to reach them – before you remove strings (save for an isolated string). When you have the strings of either type of piano removed and hung up in order you can remove the frame, for which at least two people will be needed. The upright must be on its back before you remove the frame or you may damage frame, soundboard, case and yourself seriously. Only when you have the frame out will you be able fully to assess the condition of the soundboard, and this is also the best opportunity to attend to the wrestplank and to do any work on the back and case.

Snags in Reassembly

Reassembly is largely a matter of reversing the dismantling order, but there are a few crucial stages and as I know that they can cause a good deal of wasted time, I will end with a short list.

Once you have the frame and strings on, you can do little more to soundboard and bridges. Once you have the upright's key-bed on, you cannot easily do anything to strings, bridges or soundboard. In old uprights, with pedals mounted below the bottom board, you must attend to the pedals (and the columns) whilst the piano is on its back. With actions, you must reshape hammers, whether or not in the piano, before you do final regulation, or your strike distances and set-off distances from the strings will be too large. You must set upright dampers so that, being free of the spoons and keys, they rise all together on the sustaining pedal. Do this before you try to regulate them by the damper spoons, and do not bend the damper wires once you have made this setting. Replace hammers before wippens or you will not be able to screw upright hammers into place. You must space strings evenly before you tighten a pressure bar and it is no use aligning hammers until this has been done. In grands you must check the soft pedal action and alignment with the strings before you screw on the key-blocks and replace the fall. If you are re-laying a keyboard with fresh felts, compare the height of sample keys in the piano against the key-slip, or you may find that all your keys are being balanced too high up, leaving a gap between key fronts and key-slip. Finally, you must have the piano reliably staying in tune before you attempt toning; this is perhaps the most important caution of all, for felt which is spoilt by needling in an attempt to cure a poor unison cannot be restored. Toning can do much for an old piano, but it is irreversible.

GLOSSARY OF TERMS

Note *Piano terminology is extensive and rather variable. It is believed that all the terms listed here are in common use. In some cases, however there are other words, also widely accepted, for the same things, and in some cases the definitions have been restricted according to usage in this book.*

ABSTRACT *see* PROLONGUE

AFTERTOUCH The distance which the key travels when it has ceased to drive the hammer and before it bottoms on the key-frame front rail.

AGRAFFES Studs screwed into the front (grand) or top (upright) edge of the frame next to the wrestplank. They hold the strings down so that they grip the bridge and, with the bridge, they delimit the speaking length of the strings. Restricted to the best quality pianos, and particularly so in the extreme treble.

AMPLITUDE The extent to which a string moves either side of a central straight line when vibrating.

BACK The wooden structure of beams and bracings which is the basic structure of grands and uprights.

BACK-STOP *see* BALANCE

BALANCE (BACK-STOP) A hammer-shaped projection, mounted on a short dowel in the butt of uprights' hammers. Its purpose is to meet the check. Sometimes it is fitted with a felt pad to restrict the jacks, so replacing a jack slap rail.

BALANCE PIN, BALANCE RAIL The round pin, screwed to the high central rail of the key-frame, on which the piano key is balanced.

BEARING The pressure exerted by a tensed string diverted from its natural course. Side-bearing is given by offset bridge pins, and down-bearing and up-bearing are the pressure of a string on agraffe or pressure bar or bridge.

BEATS The product of combined vibrations at different frequencies, being a throbbing vibration equal to the difference between the two frequencies. When the two frequencies are

176

too close to sound as individual notes, but not close enough to sound as a unison, there is an audible pulsation as the rarefractions and compressions of air from each source periodically coincide. This is the beat, and its frequency indicates (subject to whether the pitches are high or low) how close the two vibrations are in frequency.

BECKET The bend of the piano string as it enters the hole in the tuning pin. The word was used in the 18th century for an eyelet used to tie in a loop of rope.

BICHORD A pair of strings, of the same speaking length, tuned to the same frequency.

BLOCKING Inability of the hammer to leave a string it has struck. It is caused by the failure of the jack to escape from the hammer.

BOTTOM BOARD The plank at the bottom of an upright piano, secured to sides or toe-blocks, and to which the pedals are fitted.

BOTTOM DOOR The case panel below the keyboard in an upright piano. The bottom door has to be removed to give access to the pedal trapwork and much of the stringing.

BRIDGE Generally this is a soundboard bridge, the raised piece of wood over which the strings are stretched. Its function is to convey the strings' vibrations to the soundboard. There is a long bridge (which may be in several sections) and then a bass bridge (short bridge, overstrung bridge) for the copper-wound strings. There are also other bridges crossed by the string – notably at a pressure bar and sometimes at the hitchpin if the dead length is tuned – but confusion between the various bridges does not often arise.

BRIDLE TAPE The tape of an upright action which connects wippen and hammer and assists the return of the hammer after striking.

BRIDLE WIRES The vertical wires fixed to the wippens of upright pianos to hold the tips of bridle tapes.

BUSH, BUSHING A felt, cloth or plastic tube lining a hole, normally that for a wire or centre pin.

BUTT *see* HAMMER BUTT

CAPO D'ASTRO BAR A shaped bar in the treble of the frame in some grand pianos, which presses the string downwards after it has left the tuning pin. This is an alternative to a pressure bar or agraffes. The same corrupt Italian expression is used for a part of stringed instruments, including guitars.

CAPSTAN (DOLLY, PILOT) A fitting to each key for connecting it to the rest of the action through the wippen. Most usually an adjustable screw or felt-capped dowel running on a threaded vertical wire. There are often holes round the top of screw or dowel and the capstan is raised or lowered by means of a prod inserted into these holes; hence the name.

CARRIAGE A name for the lever assembly of the grand repetition action.

CELESTE PEDAL see PEDAL

CENTRE A pivoting point for a moving part in the piano action. The moving part has a fixed pin which pivots in bushed holes in a fixed flange.

CHECK A vertical obstruction to the return of the hammer, covered with felt or leather. It is fitted to the wippen in uprights and to the key in grands.

CHIPPING Preliminary tuning, usually be plucking with a chip of wood, after a piano has had new strings fitted. Chipping is carried out quickly by ear at about an octave below normal pitch, to impose tension gradually.

CLAVICHORD An early stringed keyboard instrument in which the strings are struck directly by metal tangents on the ends of the keys. The strings are permanently damped and vibrate only in the length from strike point to bridge, which is close to the tuning pins.

COVERED STRINGS Bass strings with hexagonal steel cores wound with one or more layers of copper wire. This is to give them mass as a compensation for their theoretical shortness.

DAMPER A shaped block of felt, mounted on a wooden head, which when it presses on a string stops it from vibrating. Grand dampers operate by gravity. Upright dampers operate by springs. Both are raised by the keys when notes are sounded, and all the dampers in the piano are raised when the sustaining pedal is depressed.

DAMPER BLOCK (DAMPER DROP, DAMPER DRUM) The cylinder of wood, attached to the damper head and carrying the fixing screw in an upright piano. In a grand piano, a similar cylinder into which the wire descending from the damper is screwed and which pivots on the damper lever.

DAMPER GUIDE RAIL A strip of thin wood with bushed holes which is mounted on the edge of a grand's soundboard to position the damper wires alongside their respective strings.

DAMPER HEAD The wooden block to which the damper felt is glued.

DAMPER LEVERS The pivoted levers, behind the action in a grand piano, to which the dampers and damper wires are attached. The same name may also be used of the pivoted block to which an overdamper is fitted in an upright piano.

DAMPER SLAP RAIL (DAMPER RAIL) A felted rail between the dampers and the main beam of an upright action. Its purpose is to limit the raising of the dampers by the sustaining pedal.

DAMPER STOP RAIL An adjustable rail screwed above the damper levers in a grand piano. Its purpose is the same as that of a damper slap rail.

DAMPER SPOON A short vertical wire, with flattened and hollowed tip, at the back of the wippen in an upright piano. The spoon is the means by which the key raises the damper when a note is struck.

DAMPER SPRINGS Springs, in graded strengths from treble (weak) to bass (strong) which press the dampers of upright pianos to the strings. Formerly of brass, now usually of steel, they considerably affect the weight of touch.

DEAD LENGTH That part of the string which does not vibrate when the string is struck, i.e. between bridge and hitchpin, and between upper bearing and tuning pin. It is usually muted by 'listing' felt or braid, but in some pianos arrangements are made to tune it proportionately to the main speaking length.

DECAY The decline of a musical note from its greatest amplitude or volume into silence. In the decay some partials may attain particular prominence and contribute to the distinctive character of the whole 'note'.

DIRECT LEVER ACTION An old type of grand action, developed from 19th-century square piano actions, in which there is no wippen and the key-mounted jack acts on the hammer butt as in upright actions. Distinguish from repetition or roller action.

DOWN-BEARING The pressure of a string on the bridge,

according to string tension and the relative height of the bridge. It may be measured in lb weight or in angles, of the string's descent from the horizontal at the top of the bridge to the upper bearing (about 15°), and from the same horizontal to the hitchpin (between 1° and 2°, with the greater in the bass). Down-bearing is one measure of the transmission of vibrations through the bridge to the soundboard and various down-bearings produce differing tonal effects.

DROP The fall of the grand hammer, from the highest point to which the jack takes it before escapement, to the height permitted by the adjustable repetition lever.

DROP SCREW (HAMMER FLANGE REGULATING SCREW) The screw, mounted in the grand hammer flange, which limits the rise of the repetition lever and which is used to adjust drop.

ENVELOPE The complete sound, including onset, decay and associated mechanical noise. On an oscillogram it is seen as a mass of waves enveloping the fundamental.

EQUAL TEMPERAMENT The process by which the harmonic series is adjusted to produce twelve equidistant semitones in an octave, in which the frequency of only one (the octave) is an integral multiple of another (the octave below).

ESCAPEMENT *see* SET-OFF

FALL The name always given to the lid which covers the keys of a piano.

FLANGE A short bracket which is shaped to fit closely over a rail in a piano action. The flange contains the bushed holes in which the centre pin of a moving part pivots.

FLY *see* JACK

FORMANT For practical purposes, the band of frequencies to which an instrument is inherently sympathetic, being less than the total frequency range of its generators. This natural resonance leads to reinforcing or clashing with elements in sounds generated (e.g. by piano strings) and so governs the tonal character of the whole instrument.

FRAME The structural bearer of piano strings' tension, now always metal and almost invariably cast iron. The frame is firmly secured to the back, and carries the hitchpins for one end of the strings, and usually also the wrestplank and tuning pins with the other end of the strings.

FREQUENCY The rate (normally cited in Hertz, cycles per second) at which a string vibrates from its rest position, to either side and back to rest. This corresponds to the pitch perceived, by a mechanism not fully understood, by the ear and brain. The speed of sound (taken to be 1,120 feet per second at average air temperature), divided by the frequency in Hertz will yield the theoretical wavelength in feet. This is not the length of string, which depends on the tension and other proportions, but strings of the same material, tension and thickness will be related in length as will their wavelengths or frequencies.

FUNDAMENTAL The natural frequency of vibration of the whole string (as distinct from partials).

GRAND A piano in which frame and strings are horizontal. The term 'upright grand' (applied to an upright claimed to be especially sonorous) is best regarded as a misnomer although it was used in the earliest years of the upright piano, as well as early in the 20th century, to impress. The horizontal grand can have, and usually does have, longer strings than the larger uprights and so 'grand', originally used to denote the remarkable pianoforte as such rather than to distinguish from the then very rare uprights, is appropriate.

HALF-BLOW ACTION A soft-pedal arrangement, usual in upright pianos, where available volume is lowered by reducing the distance of the hammers when at rest from their strings.

HALF-PEDALLING A means of sustaining the lower notes which have been played, whilst normally damped notes are played above them in the treble. It depends on the different amplitudes of vibration of the strings of various length as the dampers meet them and entails holding the sustaining pedal less than fully depressed, the exact level varying from instrument to instrument.

HAMMER, TUNING *see* TUNING HAMMER

HAMMER-BUTT The wooden block in which the hammer shanks of upright (and direct lever action grand) pianos terminate, and which is centred with a flange on the main action rail.

HAMMER FLANGE RAIL A name for the action rail to which grand hammer flanges are screwed. This is sometimes called the 'hammer rail' but may then be confused with a rail on which hammer shanks rest near the heads.

181

HAMMER RAIL The rail on which upright piano hammer shanks rest just below their heads. Sometimes also used of the rail to which grand hammer flanges are screwed.

HAMMER REST A felted rail, or blocks on to each wippen, on which grand hammer shanks either rest (direct lever action) or bounce (repetition action). Also used of the hammer rail in upright actions.

HAMMER ROLLER A nub on the shank of a hammer in the repetition action of grand pianos. It is composed of a wooden splint cushioned with felt and covered with leather, and it receives the drive from the jack, wippen and key.

HARMONIC The musical vibration of a string or part of a string (cf. FUNDAMENTAL, PARTIAL). The string vibrates as a whole and also in parts of decreasing proportion which give rise to a series of musical pitches for any one fundamental vibration, although not all the 'harmonics' may be audible. This is called the harmonic series, and the frequency of each harmonic is an integral multiple of the frequency of the fundamental.

HARPSICHORD A keyboard instrument, mainly of the 18th century, in which the strings are plucked by 'plectra' mounted on the keys. Pitch is determined by string mass and length as in the piano and strings are damped by felt attached to the keys. cf. CLAVICHORD

HERTZ The unit of frequency in cycles per second.

HITCHPINS Small pins cast into the piano frame to receive the tail ends of strings.

HOLLOW A concave beam formerly inserted in upright piano cases between the top door and the fall.

HOPPER *see* JACK

INHARMONICITY An appropriately distasteful name for the departure of the harmonic series produced by strings, from the series theoretically applying to particular lengths of string. Thus the octave partial of one string tends to be higher in pitch than the theoretical pitch of that octave note. The phenomenon, which is due to the interference of the strings' stiffness with the vibration characteristics of their length, has to be allowed for in tuning. The bigger the piano and the longer its strings, the less marked it becomes.

JACK A pivoted trigger (etymologically a 'lever') by which the key drives the hammer. Also known as a 'fly' or 'hopper'.

JACK SLAP RAIL A felted rail placed in an upright action to limit the motion of jacks after escapement. This may alternatively be performed by an extension of the balance.

KEY-BED The structural part of the case which in an upright supports the keyboard and in a grand supports keyboard and action.

KEY-BLOCKS Wooden blocks, one at either end of the keyboard. Used in grand pianos to limit the sideways motion of the action, in uprights they fill in space, with the pedal rods and stringing behind.

KEY-FRAME The wooden frame, consisting of three rails and several cross members, on which the Keyboard is laid.

KEY-SLIP A slip of wood, nowadays usually containing the lock, in front of the keyboard. In grands it must be removed before the keyboard or action can be taken out. In uprights it need not be removed and is often fixed.

LOOP STRINGING The arrangement by which two uncovered wire strings are formed from a double length of wire bent round a hitchpin. The opposite – single stringing or individual eye stringing – was formerly general and is still preferred by a very few makers.

LYRE The wooden support structure for the pedals of a grand piano. Formerly this was shaped to resemble a lyre, the various metal rods appearing as strings. This shape is now found only in reproduction work and straight tapered support columns are general.

MONOCHORD A single string and its note.

MUTE A rubber or felt wedge or strip pressed against strings to silence them during tuning.

NEEDLING *see* TONING.

ONSET The period before a musical note reaches maximum amplitude. It is characterised by partial vibrations and mechanical noise and tends to distinguish the sound of one instrument from that of another.

OVERDAMPER ACTION An upright action, now obsolete, in which the strings are damped above the strike point of the hammers. cf. UNDERDAMPER ACTION.

OVERSTRINGING The laying of the lower strings of the piano diagonally across and above the higher strings. The purpose of this is to use the more vibrant part of the soundboard and to accommodate longer strings in shorter or lower cases than would otherwise be possible.

OVERTONES *see* PARTIALS

PARALLEL STRINGING The opposite of overstringing; no strings pass over each other.

PARTIALS The vibrations of parts of the string as opposed to the whole (the fundamental). If the partials are simply proportional to the fundamental (i.e. the frequencies have an integral multiple relationship), they may be called harmonics. Practice varies in the numbering of harmonics, overtones and partials. In this book we do not distinguish, save explicitly, between partials and harmonics, and we exclude the fundamental from any count of partials.

PEDALS The following are the commoner arrangements;

Left pedal, Soft Pedal, Una Corda Pedal: reduces volume available, by one of two methods (*see* HALF-BLOW ACTION, SHIFT ACTION)

Middle Pedal: 1 Celeste, Practice Pedal: reduces volume and alters tone by interposing fabric between strings and hammers, or

2. Sostenuto Pedal: holds dampers off particular notes once they have been played.

Right Pedal, Sustaining Pedal, Loud Pedal; holds dampers off all notes for as long as it is depressed.

PEDAL NOTE A note, usually the bass of a significant chord, long sustained (particularly on the organ) whilst other notes are played above it.

PITCH The musical equivalent of frequency, i.e. the auditory sensation of relatively fast regular vibrations in the air. The higher the frequency, the faster the vibration, the higher the pitch is felt to be. The standard pitch to which instruments are nowadays related is 440 Hertz, taken to be the A above Middle C.

PITCH PIPE A basic wind instrument producing a series of standard pitches for tuning purposes.

PLATE The American name for the piano frame.

PRESSURE BAR A convex bar screwed down over the strings as they are passed over a raised bridge in the frame shortly after leaving the wrestplank. The bar ensures that the strings stay in place, that they bear on the soundboard bridges and that their speaking lengths start at a distinct and designed point. The pressure bar performs the same function as the agraffe but rather more cheaply.

PROLONGUE A wooden link between key and wippen in old large upright pianos (and in some modern small ones where the action is below the key-bed). Also known as an Abstract or Sticker.

RAIL The name given to horizontal members of the action framework and key-frame. The action rails are usually wooden, but metal rails are also used.

REGULATING BUTTON *see* SET-OFF BUTTON.

REGULATION Adjustment of the interaction of the working parts, particularly keyboard and action, to perform to accepted standards.

REPETITION ACTION The commonest action for grand pianos in modern times. It is characterized by a sprung repetition lever which can hold the hammer up for the jack to reposition itself for another blow, before the key has been fully released. Also known as 'Double Escapement Action' (perhaps because there may be two escapements for one full key action) and 'Roller Action' (because of the HAMMER ROLLER).

REPETITION LEVER The sprung lever which, in a grand repetition action, raises and holds the hammer for relocation of the jack.

REPETITION SPRING The spring which tensions the repetition lever. It is usually a double-acting spring, working also to return the jack beneath the hammer roller.

ROCKERS 1. Pivoted and sprung levers running along the bottom board of an upright piano to connect the pedals to their rods and the action, and

2. Curved blocks pivoted on to the keys for adjusting height of capstans or prolongues.

ROLLER ACTION *see* REPETITION ACTION

SAND-FILE A file made from abrasive paper stuck round a strip of wood, used for reshaping hammer felts.

SET-OFF (ESCAPEMENT) The driving of the jack away from the hammer butt or roller after which the hammer travels by momentum alone. The set-off is caused by the meeting of the fixed (but adjustable) set-off button with the heel of the jack, as the latter is raised by the depression of the key. Without escapement, the hammer would 'block' on the string and kill the sound it produced if the key were held down.

SET-OFF BUTTON A felt pad on a wooden base with an adjustable screw. This is the principal regulating device in an action. It determines when the hammer ceases to be directly impelled from the key.

SHANK The dowel, most often of hickory, which supports the hammer head.

SHARPS For piano tuners and manufacturers, these are all the black keys.

SHIFT ACTION The type of soft pedal action, usual in grand pianos, where action and keys can be moved to the right so that fewer strings than normal in each note (except monochords) are struck. This is the nearest that the modern piano comes to the instruction 'Una corda'.

SIDE-BEARING The side-pressure exerted by the string as it presses against the bridge pins which divert its course.

SINE WAVE A simple wave-form, with mathematical definition, which we can see as the pattern of a fundamental without harmonics and with equal onset and decay, the peak compression and rarefaction of the air occurring exactly halfway through each half-cycle.

SINGLE STRINGING *see* LOOP STRINGING

SOSTENUTO PEDAL *see* PEDAL.

SOUNDBOARD A wooden membrane, sealed at the edges, which amplifies (but curtails) the vibrations of the strings as transmitted through the bridges.

SPEAKING LENGTH The part of the whole string which is struck by the hammer and caused to vibrate, i.e. the string between agraffe or upper bearing, and soundboard bridge.

SPOON *see* DAMPER SPOON

STANDARDS The iron brackets which form the end and middle supports of modern upright and grand actions. Formerly, hardwood blocks were used.

STEELS All the strings which are not wound with copper wire but are simply polished steel.

STRAIGHT STRINGING (PARALLEL STRINGING) Used generally as an opposite to OVERSTRINGING. Of an upright, 'vertical'

186

or 'oblique' are sometimes used to show the plan of straight stringing.

STRETCHING OCTAVES *see* INHARMONICITY.

STRIKE DISTANCE The distance between the hammer's strike point and where it strikes the string.

STRIKE LINE The imaginary line on which the hammers strike the strings. It is usually set around the length of the strings' sixth partial (excluding the fundamental) to diminish this discordant partial.

STRIKE POINT The precise point on the hammer where it strikes the string.

STUDS *see* AGRAFFES.

TAPE CHECK ACTION The general name for the type of action which has long been in universal use in upright pianos and has bridle tapes and checks.

TOE-BLOCKS Short lengths of stout timber at the bottom of older upright pianos, supporting the columns and strengthening the join of side, back and bottom board.

TONE The musical quality of a note as governed by the number and relative strengths of fundamental and partial vibrations in the whole sound.

TONING The art of piercing hammer felts with a needle in order to alter their damping effects on the strings, and so the tone quality.

TOP DOOR The front panel of an upright piano's case, above the keyboard. The top door has to be removed to give access to the action.

TOUCH Either the manner in which the finger strikes the key; or the feel of the key and associated action to the performer. Thus 'touch' may refer to the performer or to the instrument or to both.

TRANSIENT A short-lived partial, particularly associated with the onset of a musical sound.

TRICHORD A group of three strings, of the same speaking length, tuned to the same frequency.

TUNING FORK A hard steel fork accurately cut to emit a sine wave of a given frequency when struck. Tuning forks are affected by ambient temperature and by distortion from rough handling.

TUNING HAMMER A tern applied mainly to the T-shaped

tuning lever, whose handle could formerly have been used as a hammer.

UNDERDAMPER ACTION An upright piano's modern action in which the damper damps the string beneath the strike point and as near to it as possible. cf. OVERDAMPER ACTION.

UNISON Two or more strings tuned to the same frequency and normally of the same speaking length and wire gauge.

VOICING A term, usually American, for toning in pianos, but also applied to other instruments (e.g. harpsichord, organ).

WAVELENGTH The distance, assuming the speed of sound to be 1,120 ft per second, between the beginning and end of a cycle of vibration. See FREQUENCY.

WIPPEN A pivoted lever intermediate between the key and the jack and hammer in most piano actions.

WOUND STRINGS *see* COVERED STRINGS.

WRESTPLANK A plank composed of cross-grained laminations of hardwood, usually maple, into which the tuning pins holding the strings are driven.

SELECT FURTHER READING

BRIGGS, G. A. *Pianos, Pianists and Sonics* (Wharfedale Wireless, Bradford, 1951).

FIRTH, I. *Directory of Suppliers to Craftsman Musical Instrument Makers* (Scottish Development Agency, Small Business Division, Edinburgh, 1975).

FISCHER, J. C. *Piano Tuning, A Complete Guide* (Tutor Press, Toronto, repr. 1978).

HOWE, A. H. *Scientific Piano Tuning and Servicing* (N.Y., 3rd ed., 1973).

JOHNSON, M. and MACKWORTH-YOUNG, R. *Tune and Repair Your Own Piano* (Harcourt Brace, London, 1978).

KENNEDY, K. T. *Piano Action Repairs and Maintenance* (Kaye and Ward, London, 1979).

KERZOG, K. H. *Piano-Nummern* (Verlag das Musikinstrument, 6 Frankfurt a.M., Klübestrasse 9).

NALDER, L. M. *The Modern Piano* (Unwin 1927, repr. 1977).

PIERCE, BOB *Pierce Piano Atlas* (2188 Lakewood Boulevard, Long Beach, California 9081 5).

REBLITZ, A. A. *Piano Servicing, Tuning and Repairing* (Vestal Press, N.Y. 1976).

SHEAD, H. *The Anatomy of the Piano* (Unwin, London, 1978).

SMITH, E. *Pianos in Practice, An Owner's Manual* (Scolar Press, London, 1978).

STEINWAY *Service Manual* (Steinway & Sons, N.Y., n.d.).

STEVENS, P. *Piano Tuning, Repair and Rebuilding* (Nelson Hall, Chicago, 1972).

WHITE, W. B. *Piano Tuning and Allied Arts* (Boston, Mass., 5 ed. 1946, repr. 1976).

Theory and Practice of Piano Construction (Dover, N.Y., 1906, repr. 1975).

WOLFENDEN, S. *A Treatise on the Art of Pianoforte Construction* (Unwin, London, 1916, 1927, repr. 1975).

INDEX

190